Britain
Our Way

Britain
Our Way

by Barbara Williams

Barbara Williams

Illustrated by
Dwight Williams

Dwight Williams

Library of Congress Catalog Card Number 95-71476

Williams, Barbara
Britain Our Way

ISBN 0-964-93960-6

Published by PORCH SWING BOOKS
655 E. Kingsford Drive
Meridian, Idaho 83642

Lithographed and bound in the United States of America by
The Caxton Printers, Ltd.
Caldwell, Idaho 83605

To all of our friends who travel, either in reality, or from an armchair.

Contents

INTRODUCTION

The selections in this book are not meant to suggest that certain places in Britain are more important or more visit-worthy than others. Rather, they are the result of having chosen unusual, extraordinary, or seldom-visited sites that have proved meaningful to the author and her artist husband, with a little history and illustration thrown in to tantalize others to enjoy them as well.

Occasionally we have included some very popular places, Sissinghurst Castle and Gardens or Hadrian's Wall for example, because something that we saw or experienced at those locations was particularly memorable to us. Some locations simply are places we think anyone would enjoy seeing.

We've known many people who have traveled to Britain, and out of fear of driving on the left side of the road or worry about a time element, have stayed only in London, thus missing the charm, history, and beauty of the British countryside. Americans (especially western Americans) seem to misunderstand how close things are to each other on the small island and how easily and quickly one can get from one spot to the next.

We have tried to cure the problem with the parts of this book dealing with sections of England lying south and west of London, and north into East Anglia. Even with just a few days, Wales and the areas of south-western and western England are easily reached.

If one has less than a week to spend, a quick trip out of London in any direction can be easily filled with spectacular sights. Dwight once helped some friends who had only two or three days to fill, plan an interesting sight-seeing trip south of London. They saw places they would not have seen without a little guidance. The idea was brought home to us when a lady who runs a bed and breakfast remarked, "When you meet an American, just tell him you live near either Stonehenge or the Tower of London. Those are the only things they come to see."

That is not to say that the Tower of London, Stonehenge, and other popular historical places are not interesting. Obviously they are. But in this book we would like to encourage the traveler to get outside London, away from the crowds and the most common sights to gain some understanding of history that might alter his or her perception of life in a meaningful way, just as it has altered ours. I can guarantee that these experiences will only whet the traveler's appetite to see more.

Many of the sites we have chosen are relatively unknown. Since some are hidden away in places that are not easy to find, the first rule is to have the best road map available with locations and tourist sights clearly marked on it. Maps in book form with a scale of four to five miles per inch are readily available in book shops in this country.

The first time Dwight and I visited Britain we saw the sights listed in every travel guide: Stonehenge, Tintern Abbey, the Tower of London, Westminster Abbey, Warwick Castle, Stratford-upon-Avon, Edinburgh, Loch Ness, etc. All were well worth seeing. They left us in awe of our own origins (Wales and Scotland) and with a strong desire to explore the islands more fully. The more we read, the longer our list of "must sees" became.

Five trips and thousands of photographs and paintings later (as well as many more books read and written) we are still fascinated with the United Kingdom. We keep an ongoing list of places we must see on the next trip—things historical, botanical, artistic, and literary.

Some of the places listed are difficult to fit within our specific geographic sections. If something fell between sections we placed it as accurately as possible.

Many of the national treasures in Britain are owned and kept up by The National Trust, English Heritage, or smaller trusts. Others are privately owned but open to the public for a small fee.

We have noticed lately that the locations on our list have become more obscure. Having seen the big places, we now glean out the less well-known, the novelties and small nuances that make life worth living. Often they are sites we have read or heard about that have grabbed our imagination one way or another. Chillingham Castle in Northhumberland, for instance, has kept a band of Wild White Cattle (descendants of prehistoric wild oxen) going for the past seven hundred years. Incredible!

As time passes, we concentrate more on interesting medieval villages with their winding cobbled streets, medieval buildings settled in upon themselves to withstand 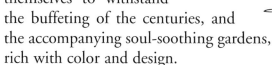 the buffeting of the centuries, and the accompanying soul-soothing gardens, rich with color and design.

While in the villages, we seldom fail to step inside the village church to admire its grandeur. Some of the earliest stained glass windows, unique architecture, carvings, and sculpture bring the past sharply into focus. Church records, kept from the villages' earliest days, are a vital part of British history. These documents are a gold mine of information for those who are of British heritage and interested in answering questions about their own family tree.

The parish churches often provide a pamphlet (selling for only a few pence) to inform the visitor of historical and artistic treasures in the church, as well as in the village. And don't forget to strike up a conversation or two with the locals. They are proud to relate facts and folklore about ancient structures and land areas in their villages.

British people are not only interesting personalities, they also possess a fantastic sense of humor. With a twinkle in their eye they'll tell you about the resident ghost of the manor house, the disguised priests' hole in the abbey, or the secret stairwell cut into the thick stone walls of the village castle.

I am reminded of the day we drove to a hamlet just north of Edinburgh called Collace (Col-ese'). It was supposed to be the site of Dunsinane, a castle mentioned in Shakespeare's *Macbeth*. We couldn't find a castle, so we stopped to ask an elderly man walking along the road.

After he had corrected our mispronunciation of the word Dunsinane (accent on the *second* syllable, Dun-sin'-an) he said, "It's up there." Bright brown eyes lit with pleasure as he pointed to the top of a hill some distance away.

We could see nothing but a sea of mud on the hillside.

"What's up there?" we asked skeptically.

"A hole," he said with pure delight.

I suppose he would have found it even more amusing if we had climbed the hill in waist-deep mud to gaze at it.

One of the questions most often asked of us is, "Where do you learn about these places?" The answer is quite simple, we read. Bookstores and libraries are full of travel books. Pick up a few, and chances are you'll find your curiosity aroused about more places than you could ever possibly have time to visit.

The English Pub is a fascination for many, so another question often asked is whether or not the English Pub is going out of style. Is it no longer the focal point of village life? There have been articles in popular magazines making such claims. The theory is that with television, the VCR, and higher prices, the British are finding their entertainment at home more than they used to.

It may be partially true. If anything, it has impressed the pub owners with the fact that they must serve better food and strengthen all-around service to compete. The old saw that British food is "bland and tasteless" is pure folklore as far as we're concerned.

We have found no dearth of pubs in Britain. With a few exceptions, the pubs marked "Free House" have better food and service since they are owned by the proprietor instead of a large national brewery. We enjoy these informal relaxing establishments where everyone feels free to join in the conversations at hand. There are still traditional games of darts and shove halfpenny to while away long winter evenings with a little folk music playing in the background.

From time to time in this book you will see a reference to the "Domesday Book" (Dooms'-day). The book was the first official census ordered drawn up in 1085-86 by William The Conqueror so he would have a detailed accounting of the land he had conquered. He then ordered territory taken from indigenous English nobility and landowners to be divided among his followers. A listing in the book generally means that there was some kind of structure on that particular piece of property in 1085. It is surprising how many of the buildings and boundaries are the same today.

When we begin to plan a trip, we decide which areas we will visit, locate the things we want to see on the map, then make a list, trying to keep sites in order to avoid backtracking. This idea certainly is helpful, but let us warn against trying to adhere too closely to a pre-planned schedule. We have never stuck entirely to our plan. Even on our last trip we decided we had been in an area long enough and made an unplanned three day detour.

On the third day of our first trip, traveling north of Bath, we saw an interesting looking village that was off the main route (and certainly not part of our plan). We whipped off the road to have a look.

The village is called Leighterton. The houses and fences glow with golden Cotswold stone. There is a church with a half-timber tower and ancient headstones in the churchyard. The caretaker unlocked the church for us, and after we had wandered through it and enjoyed a picnic on the grounds, we accepted an invitation to his home for a brief and enjoyable visit. We would hate to have missed Leighterton. The memory of that experience keeps us flexible.

Above all, in this book we want to relate in pictures and in words a montage of the enchanting variations within the United Kingdom that has captured our imagination the last few years.

Should you decide to travel to Britain, the last chapter of the book includes tips and suggestions to make your trip as enjoyable and trouble free as possible. Remember, planning is a large part of the fun. We hope our descriptions and drawings will help you make decisions about where to go and what to see.

Perhaps in your travels you will happen onto something that will appeal to us. Please let us know, and do have a wonderful time!

SOUTH OF LONDON

The area south of London is filled with some of the most interesting and ancient treasures of Britain. The Romans, beginning in the first century, built the roads and made England accessible from one side to the other. Then came the Saxons to add their piece of history in places such as Winchester, where Alfred The Great ruled. By the time the Norman Conquest was completed the area was already rife with ancient sites.

But like everything else, styles change as the centuries pass. The architecture is often a rich panoply of design spanning several centuries. The gardens, too, have undergone change from time to time.

In this section we guide you to sights from many different centuries with endless possibilities for either a few days of sightseeing, or a prolonged trip that allows you to wander with abandon.

TUDELEY

Our eye was caught one day by a brief note in a travel book about the Church of All Saints in the village of Tudeley (Tood'-ly). The small church is a rather somber structure, built of dull brown brick and stone, and shrugged off in the Domesday Book as "a church with little attendance."

The remarkable thing about it is that all around, the church contains magnificent stained glass memorial windows by the famous Russian-born artist, Marc Chagall. Pale blues, pinks, and brilliant golden yellows brighten the interior as the sun sweeps through fascinating modern designs, a decided change from the Victorian windows we so often see.

A family in the parish lost a daughter in a boating accident and engaged Chagall to create the windows in her memory. Mourning figures are depicted surrounding the drowning girl in the east window. The first of the windows was installed when Chagall was eighty years old! To be in the Tudeley Church, especially on a sunny day, is a glorious experience of color.

And to think, all of this is in an unassuming little church used for munitions storage during the Second World War.

CHAGALL WINDOW TUDELEY

1

DWIGHT
WILLIAMS
- MOAT AND BRIDGE AT GROOMBRIDGE MANOR -

GROOMBRIDGE

One evening, after several unsuccessful attempts to find lodging along the East Sussex-Kent border, we inquired at a sixteenth-century half-timber in Groombridge called The Crown Inn. If you can imagine a wheezing, back-broken, ancient building with sign blown askew described as romantic, then you have a perfect idea of the Crown Inn.

We obtained a room and soon discovered that the floor dropped downhill at the ratio of approximately twelve inches per six feet. The bed was propped up with slabs of wood on one end to level it. What a strange experience it was to get up in the night and find ourselves running downhill in the dark with a total loss of equilibrium. But the food was excellent and the innkeeper fascinating. He was interested in our backgrounds and would not hear of our leaving without seeing Dwight's slides of British paintings.

After reviewing the slides, with an abundance of pride he insisted we see the village's manor house (might Dwight paint it?), a grand Restoration country house called GROOMBRIDGE PLACE. The interior panelling was reused from the Elizabethan manor which had once stood on the site. The old moat, planted with ramblers and lush foliage, was kept for its decorative qualities, blending nicely with the seventeenth-century stone-walled garden.

CHARTWELL

I should think that anyone who travels south of London would want to pay a visit to Chartwell, Sir Winston Churchill's country home.

The three-story red brick house contains many of Churchill's original belongings and is steeped in an unshakable aura of history. An original Monet painting hangs over a game table set up in the living room for Sir Winston's favorite game of bezique. In his study, a map on the wall diagrams the Mulberry project related to the 1944 invasion of Normandy.

One can almost feel Churchill's presence in the museum of memorabilia. It is a collection of articles given to him during World War II by leaders from all over the world. An enormous battle-scarred Nazi flag, with its ominous swastika, once waved brazenly from a busy German tank. Stopping us in our tracks, the flag caused us to consider anew what Churchill must have been up against in his battle against Hitler.

I suppose the reason we felt history so keenly at Chartwell is because World War II took place during our lifetime, and Churchill has always been one of our heroes. The events are things we can clearly recall. We don't have to imagine them.

Away from the house is a studio filled with Churchill's paintings—some good, some probably not so good. But it is simply fascinating to realize that during the Second World War Churchill was not only running his country and trying to defeat Germany, he also wrote extensively on the history of the English language and *still* found time to paint.

One of Churchill's distractions from the pressing world of politics and writing was building high brick walls. They enclose impressive grounds, including a well-designed Oriental lily pond and an attractive rose garden. Beside a larger pond behind the house there is a provocative white wooden chair. There Churchill often sat while contemplating his monumental responsibilities. Perhaps it is just as well that he is not around to see the terrible devastation of the woods above the pond caused by heavy windstorms in recent years.

Behind the house is a pergola entwined with climbers that shade chairs and potted plants. It is a nostalgic spot from which to ponder the past.

D.W. BEST BEECH

BEST BEECH PUB

A British truism is that a pub lives or dies on the personality of the innkeeper. So quite often the pub is the best place for a little local color, and more often than not it is the best place to eat supper. The Best Beech Pub in an area just west of Wadhurst called Mark Cross Hill, is a good example.

The bartender was a popular chap and well-acquainted with his clientele. When he saw certain of his regular customers coming in the early evening he mixed odd-combination drinks for them. The customers, regulars, all sniffed at the drink and tried to guess what the ingredients were. While the victim drank the concoction with gusto (accompanied by good cheer from his friends), he reluctantly dug in his pockets to pay for it. The bartender's innocent dead-pan expression added charm to the occasion.

It's always fun to watch a group have a good time, and it was enough to keep us returning to Best Beech Pub for several evenings while we were in the area.

Consider the BRITISH PUB in general. A unique thing about pubs (actually "Inn" is a more nearly correct title) is not only looking over the timeless buildings that house many of them, but discovering the array of collections they have garnered through the years. Each pub has its individual collection of antique or otherwise interesting items—often hung between ceiling beams, up and down walls, and across the mantles of massive fireplaces. We have seen beer and ale mugs, foreign (and sometimes very old) money, ale and milk pitchers, wine glasses, horse brasses, Toby jugs, and blue and white oriental china pieces. One had a highly desirable antique clock collection. Antique prints of dogs, hunting scenes, horse races and jumps, and famous racing cars and their drivers are also popular. Often collections reveal interest in local geology, sports, or industry.

"There is no way to emulate the English Pub," one innkeeper told us. "It is a way of life that has involved the entire community from early medieval times. Other countries try to copy it but they have not proven themselves effective, and they never will."

To my knowledge, the oldest inn we have visited was one called THREE CHIMNEYS in a village by the same name a few miles from Sissinghurst. The inn was built in 1420 and is one of the few that has remained the same throughout the centuries—anything-but-straight low-beamed ceilings, beer kegs on a low bench behind the bar, very low headers over the doors (ouch! When I have to duck at five-feet-two-inches, heaven help the rest of you), and antique horse brasses spread at random across the fireplace, set the visitor back in history to a time when necessity was far more important than decor.

Many of the inns bear animal names—The Swan, The Hart. Bulls, Horses, and Dogs, all of various colors and descriptions are popular, such as The Wensley Dale Heifer, The Bear & Ragged Staff, The Cat and Fiddle, The Ancient Unicorn. Lore has it that from under the sign of an inn called The Cock and another nearby in the same village called The Bull arose the ale-induced tall tales we know as the "cock and bull" stories.

We've met some very interesting people in these colorful inns. One lady bartender, scarcely a hundred miles west of London, told us she had no use for "that trafficky city of London. I went there once many years ago. I didn't like it and I've never been back!" This may seem like a strange attitude, but it doesn't take long to realize that people in Britain simply don't travel the distances we do. An hour's drive is the most many of them will opt for over narrow winding lanes. Some of it may be a holdover from the days when villages were entities unto themselves and outsiders coming and going were a threat.

With the knowledge that pubs sometimes change hands (and not always for the better), I list some of our favorites from over the years. These are pubs not otherwise mentioned in the book:

Windmill Inn, Cranbrook, Kent
Fox and Hound Inn, Tytherington, Wiltshire
Crossways Inn, Folly Gate, Devon
Bailey's Wine Bar, Bridgnorth, Shropshire
George and Dragon, Newton, Norfolk
Maypole Inn, Long Preston, North Yorkshire
The Bay Horse Inn, Rainton, North Yorkshire

SISSINGHURST CASTLE.

D.W.

SISSINGHURST CASTLE AND GARDENS

East of Groombridge through Royal Tunbridge Wells is Sissinghurst, the location of one of England's best known and best loved world-class gardens. "I wish everybody had a garden, and would work in it himself," Anna Warner, a writer of gardening books in America once wrote. "The world would grow sweeter-tempered at once."

Sissinghurst gardens were laid out in 1930 by the famous gardener, Vita Sackville-West, in a formal style with Elizabethan small enclosures that contain either a limited type of plant, such as old-fashioned rose varieties, or blooms of all one color, such as all white or all blue. Our favorite was the White Garden. The combination of silver and blue-gray foliage with all white blooms in varying heights and shapes is outstanding.

We hope you have more luck with a white garden than we had. We've found that before long a pretty soft pink rose or a bright clematis we simply can't resist creeps in to foil the scheme.

The fascinating things about English gardens like Sissinghurst are the rich display of heavy bloom in perennial borders backed by a profusion of climbing clematis and roses; the array of unusual patinated tubs and pots crammed with ferns and ramblers; thick yews trimmed into delightful topiary in just the right places to enhance height and space; and long rows of hedges ending in sun-and-shade-dappled glens that reveal a lovely cast-iron bench or sculpture at the end as an unexpected surprise.

GREAT DIXTER

Great Dixter is a fifteenth-century half-timbered manor house with an unusual history. Another half-timber was bought, taken apart and carefully marked, then moved to the site where it was put back together and joined to the original Dixter house. The architect, Sir Edwin Lutyens, accomplished the feat admirably in 1910. Historians have called the project "a perfect marriage."

But as lovely and unusual as the house is, Great Dixter is probably as well known for its wide range of plants, flowers, striking sweeps of perennial borders, and unusual topiary, also laid out by Lutyens. (I mean, where else would you find topiary chocolate pots?)

Let's face it, our steady diet of petunias, geraniums, and marigolds in the States is pure boredom and lack of imagination, so if you have a green thumb (green fingers in Britain), give yourself plenty of time to examine the plant labels and take notes in this famous garden, for you're sure to be encouraged to match some of the showy blooms with which you are not now familiar.

Some of the gardens offer seed packets in their gift shops. Surprisingly, we find that many of the plants we see in Southern England grow every bit as well in the western United States. (Do add a little water!)

DWIGHT WILLIAMS

GREAT DIXTER, KENT

PETWORTH. W. SUSSEX.
DWIGHT WILLIAMS

PETWORTH AND PETWORTH HOUSE

This small town north of Arundel is recorded in the Domesday book as "a fine example of a medieval market town." An amazing variety of antique shops gathered around a network of narrow cobbled streets keeps you looking for "special finds" for days on end if you're so inclined. The owners of the shops are friendly and accommodating and will cooperate with other shops to pack purchases and ship them to you in the United States in a shared container.

An added attraction is PETWORTH HOUSE, famous for its spectacular gateway (taller than most buildings in town at one time, they claim), and a large collection of J. M. W. Turner's oil paintings. The gate into the property is easy to find on the edge of town.

The thing we found astonishing about the house was not the Turner paintings, but the magnitude of the intricate wood carvings in "The Carved Room" done by the seventeenth-century craftsman, Grinling Gibbons. Fruits, birds, and flowers entwined with a variety of leaves and tendrils seem to twist and curl around every available upright, travel around massively-framed portraits, and crawl onto the picture moulding beneath the cove of the ceiling. Rising in the cove over the moulding are lacy carved pediments.

The village of Petworth was, to us, more interesting and enjoyable than Petworth House. We have returned to enjoy the village several times.

THE GARDEN & POND.
BATEMAN'S

BATEMAN'S

God gives all men all earth to love,
　But, since man's heart is small,
Ordains for each one spot shall prove
　Beloved over all.
Each to his choice, and I rejoice
　The lot has fallen to me
In a fair ground—in a fair ground—
　Yea, Sussex by the sea!

Rudyard Kipling wrote these words when he returned to his beloved Sussex home, Bateman's, to begin the last phase of his literary career in 1902. Indeed, the poem is entitled "Sussex." You'll find the house southwest of Burwash. It is a gabled seventeenth-century home of fine proportions with outstanding eighteenth-century furnishings. On the grounds is a watermill adapted by Kipling to provide his own electricity for the house.

Upstairs, his study is preserved just as he left it; a quaint desk backed by wood panelling under a window that looks onto the gardens below; a well-used globe within arm's reach of his chair; an old typewriter that looks as though it had done its share to help write those many pages of verse, short stories, and novels; a beamed ceiling and oriental rugs to add to the overall warmth and charm of the room. We assume he did well for a writer of his time since the block-long Rolls Royce he drove is still parked in the garage.

The grounds are well laid out, from the roses and clematis scrabbling over each other for a spot on the entry walls, to the colorful flower-lined walkways and the large double lily pond alive with koi and aquatic greens in the side lawn.

Whether or not you're a Kipling fan, you'll find Bateman's a distinctive residence. Some of our favorite places to visit and photograph are those of literary characters, artists, and musicians. Britain's pride in its historical artists of all kinds never wavers.

TEA is a British institution, something to eat and drink (coffee is gaining in popularity) around 4:00 p.m. Food historians believe tea may have been introduced into England by way of Japan rather than China as once believed. It made its debut as a medicinal drug in the early sixteen hundreds—an herb thought to fend off many common ailments. It soon became a popular drink.

Often tea is what we might consider a small meal. Sandwiches, fruits and sweets are served. It is wise to take advantage of a good snack, since dinner is rarely served anywhere in Britain before 7:00 p.m., and often much later.

The fun thing about stopping for tea each afternoon is that every teahouse is different. It might be housed in anything from the corner of a made-over cow barn to an elegant carriage house, a bench in a garden, a grandly decorated Victorian parlor, or possibly in a country house's giant-size kitchen amongst a full display of intricately-rigged cooking devices and a random collection of unbelievably large copper cooking pots. As you travel, take time now and then for a cup of tea. I mean, that's partly what your travels are about—local customs—isn't it?

STANDEN HOUSE

Standen is a nineteenth-century house built around a medieval structure. William Morris, possibly the most famous member of the Pre-Raphaelite Arts and Crafts movement, designed some of the furnishings and most of the busy but handsome textiles, wallpapers, and carpets. Many of them are original while others have been faithfully reproduced from the original patterns. The house contains its original electric light fixtures that suggest early art deco. The late nineteenth-century interiors are an interesting contrast to most of the other big houses that are eighteenth century at the latest, and often early medieval.

A terraced garden with comfortable garden houses and a wide lawn with fine old trees offer a panoramic view of the Weir Wood Reservoir glistening with reflected light in the distance.

ALFRISTON

Alfriston, the charming half-timbered Old Clergy House dating from 1350 was the first building acquired by the National Trust in 1896. The cost? Ten pounds. The house is an unassuming partially tile-hung structure with a thatched roof, leaving the underthatch visible inside.

A pretty, typically English perennial garden with both formal and informal areas surrounds the house.

The Church of St. Andrews perches on a rise of ground above the Clergy House. It contains a twentieth-century stained glass Jesse window (traces the genealogy of Christ through picture back to David and his father, Jesse).

DWIGHT WILLIAMS.

WEALD HOUSE, SINGLETON, W. SUSSEX.

WEALD AND DOWNLAND OPEN AIR MUSEUM

At a bed and breakfast in Fittleworth, near Petworth, our host assured us we would enjoy the Weald and Downland outdoor Museum. We knew nothing about it, but after seeing it, we were glad we had taken his advice.

The museum, located south of Petworth at Singleton, preserves many ancient styles of buildings, methods of labor, and old breeds of animals. You'll need to allow time to walk over several acres to see everything—how Tudor half-timber houses were built, how charcoal was made, as well as a display on how to thatch a roof. An extensive collection of medieval and later buildings were saved from demolition and rebuilt on the site—several Weald houses and an early half-timbered market house infilled with brick.

With a better understanding of ancient crafts, the stroll is finished at a nice little teahouse on the grounds for a rest, a cup of tea, and a "sweet."

DWIGHT
WILLIAMS
GREAT HALL · ARUNDEL CASTLE.

ARUNDEL CASTLE

We had not given Arundel Castle any more thought than simply a place to visit until it erupted before us through an English morning mist like something from the pages of an enchanting fairy tale. When you consider it, the high chalky hump above the River Arun created a strategic location from which to guard the Arun Valley against invasions from the Continent.

The castle was begun during the reign of Edward the Confessor. The crenellated keep, barbican, and the draw-bridge all date from Norman times.

The castle has a stormy history. In 1643 it was besieged by Cromwell's troops and partially destroyed by cannon fire. In the eighteenth and nineteenth centuries the various Dukes of Norfolk, who still own the property, restored the build-ings.

The fairy tale feeling is intensified when one enters the dining room, a breathtaking room with floor-to-ceiling Gothic lancet windows, smooth flagstone floors, a gigantic stone fireplace flanked by imported oriental blue and white ginger jars, and wrought iron candle-laden chandeliers hang-ing on long black chains from a thirty-foot ceiling.

What a pleasure it would be to dine with elegance at the ancient china-and-silver-set dining table while a glowing fire danced shadowy wraiths into dark corners, setting the stage for one to enjoy a delightful English meal in a room steeped with history and a tinge of fear of the past.

Forced to settle for reality instead, we had tea in the cas-tle tea garden. After our visit I learned that the beautiful din-ing room had once been a chapel.

MOTTISFONT ABBEY AND GARDENS

In Mottisfont Abbey Gardens we felt we were standing in a Monet painting, wrapped around with the tantalizing luxury of beautiful colors while the intoxicating scent of old roses filled the air.

The gardens are not exceptionally large. From the way the roses spilled from the beds and scrambled over classical arbors, pillars, and walls, we thought every species of old European rose in cultivation today must be represented. But we were wrong. There are three hundred varieties in the garden, but the gardeners claim the collection is not yet complete. This is a garden to meander through. Every plant is labeled, and there are knowledgeable gardeners working about the place to answer the public's questions.

We found the lovely old roses to have prettier color and shape, and in many cases, a livelier scent than the odorless overblown tea roses one finds in the shops and catalogs these days.

We spent two afternoons taking photographs and notes, hoping to add interesting varieties to our own new rose garden. Some varieties will not be easily found, but we're always willing to do some searching.

While I sauntered through the garden, I came on a handsome elderly woman sitting on one of the wrought iron benches. A lovely print dress was topped by a mauve afternoon hat that matched a winsome drift of mauve and white flowers nearby.

"You should sit in that spot all afternoon," I said wistfully, admiring her beauty. "Your hat matches the garden perfectly."

She looked up at me, smiled, and in her most cultured British speech said, "We do try hard, you know."

Her answer should have come as no surprise to me. I know how seriously the British take their gardening image. Later I pulled her in with my telephoto lens from across the garden. For some reason she had kept her eye on me, for she looked straight at me and smiled for the camera.

We couldn't get in the abbey (an Augustinian structure made into a mansion after the dissolution) since The National Trust was refurbishing it. The Trust, as well as other groups involved with restoration, close some of the historic houses and castles from time to time for large-scale renovation. Enclosing the place in scaffolding and plastic, they give it anything from a cleaning to a total facelift. Some of the older buildings may need major shoring-up, or possibly a new lead or slate roof that could require years to replace. The traveler learns to put up with these inconveniences, knowing that another important historic site will be saved to see at another time.

SALISBURY CATHEDRAL

After seeing Salisbury Cathedral it has been difficult for us to develop a full appreciation for other cathedrals. We have visited many others, but Salisbury remains the most beautiful to our hearts and eyes.

Inside, stunning full-length stained glass east windows brush the shadowy interior with mellow blues and reds. The main decorative elements are dark marble columns carved to represent foliage.

It is the only cathedral in England that was built in the Middle Ages as a single concept rather than its construction having been spread over centuries. The foundations were laid in 1220 and work was finished within forty years. Only the tall spire, topping out at 404 feet, was added later. A grand medieval gateway leads the visitor to the grounds.

A medieval stone frieze of biblical characters above the arcading in the Chapter House is considered one of the finest examples of medieval carving in England.

The Cathedral's greatest treasure is ownership of one of the three originals of the Magna Carta, signed at Runnymede in 1215. The priceless document has been housed in the Cathedral since 1225. Over the centuries, Salisbury has become the guardian of a valuable collection of illuminated (fancifully decorated) medieval manuscripts and early printed books and documents. A display of early silver vessels on loan from parish churches is a thought-provoking collection.

Before you pay the Cathedral a visit, you might find it rewarding to read the historical novel, *Sarum*, by Edward Rutherford. It documents the area around Salisbury from prehistory, the building of the Cathedral after the See was moved from Old Sarum (you can visit ruins of the early town nearby), to the present Cathedral in New Sarum, or Salisbury.

DWIGHT WILLIAMS -The Pergola at Mompesson House. Salisbury

In the close at Salisbury is MOMPESSON HOUSE, a fine house of the eighteenth century. It contains an elegant oak staircase, period furnishings, and an important collection of eighteenth-century drinking glasses along with other fine china. A pretty walled garden is distinguished by a classical pergola with wisteria and climbing roses. When we visited, the house was being prepared for the filming of *Sense and Sensibility* by Jane Austen. Hugh Grant and Emma Thompson are the stars.

OTHER THINGS TO SEE

While in the area drive through small villages such as EAST DEAN, WEST BURTON, and SUTTON to admire ancient rubblestone churches, the countryside, and colorful farmhouses and their gardens. The village of BIGNOR has Roman ruins.

In UPWALTHAM, a twelfth-century parish church is worth seeing. In the twelfth century there were but two rooms in the churches, the long narrow nave, and an apse at the east end just large enough to accommodate an altar—a much simpler plan than the thirteenth and fourteenth-century designs. You'll have to look for this attractive little church. It is situated on a hill in a pasture with nothing more than a grassy path leading into it.

ROYAL TUNBRIDGE WELLS is known for its mineral baths enjoyed by royalty from about 1606. The Pantiles, a handy shopping center, is famous for its antique shops and specialties in both food and gifts.

MANOR FARMHOUSE
FLISHINGHURST. KENT

SOUTHWEST ENGLAND

Many of our favorite country houses are in the Southwest of England—Manor houses distinguished by the fact that they were owned and lived in by the Lord of the Manor, and houses privately owned by country gentlemen and titled families.

There is no doubt in the historian's mind that these enormous and often exquisitely lavish homes were originally built to display the owner's wealth. While some are still privately owned, many have been turned over to the National Trust or other maintenance organizations because the families could no longer afford the financial burden of upkeep and taxes.

In this section we have listed several big houses we have enjoyed. Each has its own style of architecture and decorative elements.

Through Wiltshire, Somerset, Dorset, Devon, and Cornwall, a plethora of prehistoric stone circles, long cairns (monuments built of stone) and burial barrows scatter across the landscape. Prehistoric camp sites in this area have been dated as early as 9000 B.C.

As the traveler works his way across the southwest, he might keep in mind a piece of advice given to us by a local, "Don't just rush through this country on your way to Cornwall, it's beautiful." And indeed it is. These shires share high moor country—Exmoor, mostly in Somerset, Dartmoor in Devon, and Bodmin Moor in Cornwall—bare plateaus that suddenly widen into lush valleys and sheltered estuaries on both the channel and the north coast. They are as picturesque today as they were centuries ago.

Cornwall enjoys a unique character in England. It is one of the few spots remaining in the world today that made up the original small Celtic world (Brittany in France, Cornwall, Wales, Ireland, and Scotland). Its fishing villages closely resemble Celtic villages along the shores of Ireland and Scotland.

DWIGHT
WILLIAMS
~LACOCK, WILTSHIRE.

LACOCK, VILLAGE AND ABBEY

Exceptional dedication has saved the Augustinian nunnery at Lacock, founded in 1232, from destruction. It has been ranked as one of the most visit worthy of all of England's monastic sites.

There are those of us who might argue with that theory, but perhaps it is realistic when one realizes that the abbey was turned into a country mansion after 1539 with a minimum

of alteration to its original convent buildings. Several original walls and three provocative fifteenth-century cloister walks still stand.

The great barn near the abbey houses the Fox Talbot museum of photography (including the first recognizable photograph he made), for it was here that Talbot perfected his calotype technique to lay the foundations for modern photography.

The village has exquisite weathered Cotswold stone houses from the fifteenth century and is every photographer's dream. Of special interest is the huge tithe barn near the village center. Close scrutiny of the interior roof timbering will fascinate those interested in early construction methods.

CASTLE COMBE

Castle Combe was once dubbed "the prettiest village in England." There is no question that it is a pretty village, with its golden Cotswold-stone cottages hung with bright baskets of flowers cascading between stone-mullioned windows.

A steep-roofed fifteenth-century market cross is the spot where goods were traded on market day. Some villages still call them "butter crosses."

Like many of the villages in the Cotswolds, Castle Combe is a favorite tourist spot. I suppose nearly everyone who visits the village has his photo snapped on the hump of the famous pack bridge spanning the River ByBrook. Not long after we visited the village we saw a magazine ad showing an expensive sports car, driven by a beautiful young woman, crossing the Castle Combe bridge.

This village was once the center of cloth weaving and claims to have added the word "blanket" to the English language. It seems that the Blanket Brothers, who were weavers, devised the covering for their own bed. The name stuck.

A large, historical faceless clock in the church tower at Saint Andrews chimed the time out over the area for the field hands many years ago. Apparently they didn't need to see its face, only hear it s chime.

After looking over the town and browsing through antique shops, the visitor can locate one of the beautifully furnished tea rooms and have "a nice cup of tea with clotted cream."

BERKELEY AND BERKELEY CASTLE

The castle, begun in 1163, has been the home of a succession of Berkeleys (Bar'-clay) for more than eight hundred years. Its walls, turrets, and towers that were ominous to the onlooker centuries ago, were a haunting sight to us as the changing shadows of late afternoon flowed over its three glowing blood colors of stone.

The thing that originally sent us to visit Berkeley Castle was historical. King Edward II was brutally murdered there in 1327 when his wife and her lover plotted against him. The room in which he was imprisoned and finally tortured to death has been kept intact. A deep dungeon where prisoners were starved to death is near the murder room.

That, of course, is the castle's gruesome side. Sometimes, when we show slides of Berkeley, someone always says, "I don't want to see that kind of ugliness." Our opinion is that history is history and the more we know about it the better off we are.

On the bright side, inside the castle is a Long Drawing Room with gilded furniture, a nice Picture Gallery, and a magnificent oak-beamed, stone-floored Great Hall. It has been used many times for colorful location in television plays and movies.

One of the many pleasures of our visit was meeting a friendly couple from Bristol who invited us to tea in the castle courtyard. We learned that they have friends in Idaho.

Edward Jenner, the man who discovered that vaccination prevents communicable diseases, was born in and worked in BERKELEY VILLAGE. He was the first to recognize that milkmaids who had contracted mild cowpox were immune to smallpox. His work grew from that discovery.

The day we were at the castle a wedding had just taken place at the village church nearby. The bride and groom were "dressed to the nines" in white Victorian wedding clothes with a decorated Rolls Royce waiting to whisk them away to an unknown destination. The happy pealing of the church bells and the handsome young couple filled with hopes for the future added a sparkle to our day.

DWIGHT WILLIAMS

HARDY'S COTTAGE.

HIGHER BOCKHAMPTON

We had an enjoyable early morning stroll through sun-dappled beech woods accompanied by a rousing chorus of unfamiliar bird song to reach Greenwood Home at Higher Bockhampton, the birthplace of novelist and poet, Thomas Hardy. The thatched cottage, built in 1800 by his great grandfather, must be a prototype of the romantic notion of thatched English cottages often pictured in children's story-books. It nestles at the edge of the peaceful woods, seeming to grow naturally from the landscape.

We were greeted in the front garden by the resident striped tabby, who purred with delight to have yet one more pair of visitors come by to sigh over his fairy tale house and gardens. The house has been little altered since it was built and is viewed inside by appointment only.

The loosely-knit garden spreads across the front of the house and is anchored by a prominent bright magenta rhododendron. Beneath it a quilt of flowers decorates the beds—delphiniums, bright poppies, foxglove, and other perennials that keep a variety of colorful blooms blazing throughout the summer. There is nothing more beautiful than an English garden allowed to have its own way.

This is a restful place where the visitor is content to snap a photo or two, then simply stand back and enjoy the classic English beauty of it all.

A selective quote from *Tess of the D'Urbervilles* explains Hardy's feelings about his beloved Wessex: "The Village of Marlott lay amid the north-eastern undulations of the beautiful Vale of Blackmoor....an engirdled and secluded region, for the most part untrodden as yet by tourist or landscape painter....a fertile and sheltered tract of country, in which the fields are never brown and the springs never dry...a broad rich mass of grass and trees, mantling minor hills and dales...."

The small hamlet of HIGHER BOCKHAMPTON has other nice cottages and gardens. The folks here, we noticed, are proud of their garden fences, to the point of perhaps making it a contest. Several different styles caught our attention, some of willow branches woven into very intricate basket-weave patterns that lined the front of the property and were at least six feet high—a time-consuming project.

After drinking in the simple beauty of the area, the walk back through the woods to the car park is slower with a savoring of the wild woods that weave a quiet country tapestry through Hardy's writings.

ATHELHAMPTON

An old maxim says that the British house is in the city, but the home is in the country. While most of us do not live quite so elaborately, one of the joys of touring lovely old country homes is that they give us ideas that work on a smaller scale in our own home. We have found many ideas that enhance our home with simple but elegant touches. All European and Asian aspects of design are represented in British country homes, so you can draw from any type of architecture and design that pleases you.

This was all brought home to us with a visit to ATHELHAMPTON HALL.

It glowed like a piece of polished amber in the afternoon sun. This Elizabethan gentleman's country home is of modest scale, but is every bit as beautiful as the grand-scale houses, and, I would guess, far more practical and comfortable. It is built around a small stone-paved courtyard with an extended two-story front entrance. Although the rooms are quite large and high-ceilinged, wood panelling, wide oak-planked floors, and timber roofs create warmth inside. The Great Chamber has heraldic-patterned stained glass windows and seventeenth-century plasterwork ceilings.

Outside, golden stone is set off by dark green yews clipped in the traditional Elizabethan manner, while hordes of glossy green ramblers pull together the home's irregular design, such as heavy dormers that are not aligned with the lower windows, and a section of the house that splays out from the corner instead of turning at a right angle. This lack of symmetry adds to the overall attractiveness.

And then there is the giant croquet court around a pond in the side lawn. How civilized!

DWIGHT WILLIAMS
- ATHELHAMPTON HALL, DORSET. -

22

AVEBURY AND MALMESBURY

After tipping our hats to Stonehenge (there is always a crowd, and the site is now guarded by chain link fences and dogs), we moved on down the road a few miles to the less well-known, but older and just as fascinating, stone circle of AVEBURY. We passed SILBURY HILL, a man-made mound 130 feet high dating from at least 2500 B.C. No one knows its purpose.

There is mystery in the ancient grey stones encircling the village of Avebury as well, encircling like stone soldiers placed on a battlefield. A site for pagan rituals, or a temple to worship the sun? Archaeologists have puzzled over it for centuries. Whatever its purpose, they figure the circle was set up at least two hundred years before Stonehenge, which dates somewhere around 3500 B.C. The heaviest of the stones weighs about forty tons, with several having shapes that suggest human figures. A long avenue of more stones leading to the circles, and extensive earthworks, complete the prehistoric site.

The VILLAGE OF AVEBURY sets within the twenty-seven-acre double ring of stones. It has a sixteenth-century Norman church, a handsome thatched barn from the seventeenth century, and a lovely manor house set under spreading beech trees.

We didn't go into the house. Somehow it seemed trivial after contemplating the ancient stone circles.

MALMESBURY ABBEY, WILTSHIRE – NORMAN CROSSING ARCHES. →

Before leaving this area, stop at MALMESBURY'S twelfth-century Benedictine abbey to see the splendid medieval stone carvings of the Apostles under vaulting on the east and west walls of the porch. It is considered some of the finest stonework to survive from the twelfth century. A portion of the original abbey is used as a parish church and houses the tomb of the Saxon king, Athelstan.

Beautiful weeping copper beech trees, shining like new pennies in the sun, sway caressingly around and through the arched ruins. The trees seem to need the rainy climate of Britain to do well since the variety cannot be found in the dry climate of the western United States. They pop out of the greenery throughout Britain, but somehow they are at their loveliest on the grounds of Malmesbury.

DWIGHT
WILLIAMS
~GARDEN HOUSE,
MONTACUTE ~

The Nine Worthies are carved on the east front of the house. Inside, fine plasterwork, ornate wood panelling, and beautifully-carved fireplaces are witness to the care taken in building these fine old country homes. A gallery runs the whole length of the second floor. Unlike many mansions that have a collection of dark family portraits of mixed quality, the long gallery at Montacute has a collection of outstanding sixteenth-century portraits from the National Portrait Gallery.

We thought the house was fascinating, one that anyone would enjoy seeing. The gardens are well manicured with unusual statuary and fine yew topiary. Don't leave until you've strolled the grounds and have seen the grand oriel window on the end of the house high above the formal gardens.

MONTACUTE HOUSE

We need only glance at Montacute House, all bright topaz Ham stone glittering with glass, to recognize it as one of the finest Elizabethan mansions in England, although not as well known as some others.

The house, completed in 1600, stands on the grounds of a twelfth-century Cluniac priory. The battlemented priory gatehouse survives.

DARTMOOR SCENERY

The River Tamar separates Devon from Cornwall. In Devon, the high rocky crags of Dartmoor move south to seaside sand. The Moor is known for its sudden-enveloping ocean mist that can take a menacing turn for the unsuspecting.

We found the Moors to be quite friendly, even in the wind and rain, and thoroughly enjoyed the herds of wild Dartmoor ponies that freely roam the area.

Acres of oak and birch woodland and moorland along with wide velvety patches of planted conifers make up a National Nature Reserve. Nature trails and miles of woodland paths are available for walkers. We found it amazing that a small island about the size of the State of Oregon can keep such vast undeveloped areas with some fifty million population to use it.

In the eighteen hundreds, horsedrawn tramways carried building stone from the high Moorlands. Closed tin mines produced many relics of the industrial revolution.

CASTLE DROGO, a modern castle designed and built by Sir Edwin Lutyens in 1910, is of interest to many travelers. It is found near the northeastern edge of Dartmoor. I suppose the first question we all ask ourselves is, "Why would a person want to build a baronial-looking fortress in the twentieth century?" I don't know the answer, but I would guess that living around many old castles with their heroic history carries such a romantic vision that some people want to relive it with modern comforts.

DARTMOOR PONIES

To our eyes Lutyens seems to have attempted a mixture of the medieval and art deco at Drogo. It may sound like a weird idea but he made it work.

If you enjoy photography, or if you simply want to look at grand scenery, plan to take some extra time crossing Dartmoor.

DWIGHT
WILLIAMS
— COTEHELE HOUSE,
CORNWALL —

COTEHELE HOUSE

Just inside Cornwall on the west edge of Dartmoor is COTEHELE (Co-tel'), a fifteenth-century granite-built house considered one of the least-altered examples of a medieval squire's home.

An evocative ramble through this seemingly endless house produces a Great Hall with an arch-braced roof and a massive collection of armour on the walls, recalling a time when the communal life of the Middle Ages echoed throughout. Many smaller rooms radiate from the hall and contain original furnishings and needlework. Upstairs, surprisingly ornate bedrooms are furnished with oak pieces and grand four-poster beds.

The gardens came later, since gardens of the fifteenth century tended to be only utilitarian and woods were never built near a home that might be subject to raid. Today, unusual hand-built stone benches give the colorful formal gardens (set on several levels) a rustic touch. Lush woodsy plantings steep the rest of the grounds in eye-catching greenery.

This is a romantic house that captured our imagination. I think, even today, a family could live quite comfortably in it.

DWIGHT
WILLIAMS
~GWEEK BOATYARD
CORNWALL ~

GWEEK

The name itself snared us. On our way to Frenchman's Creek, we dropped south from the Poldark Mine to the Lizard Peninsula, where the small village of Gweek lies at the head of the Helford Estuary.

It's hard to believe that this slumbering village was once a busy port (there are still boats of one kind or another strewn about), providing imported supplies for the tin mines to the north. The port silted up, leaving a quiet scatter of cottages behind with little left to remind modern residents of the village's early importance. A very old, well-used stone bridge near the village inn is the one thing that still anchors the area to the past.

Nearby, a SEAL SANCTUARY that treats sick or injured seals before they are returned to the sea may be of interest to some.

JAMAICA INN & FRENCHMAN'S CREEK

We have so thoroughly enjoyed Daphne du Maurier's novels about Cornwall that we went to see the locations she wrote about in *Jamaica Inn* and *Frenchman's Creek*. Could the area possibly have been so full of wreckers, pirates, and beautiful young women with loose ends to their lives?

We first stopped at JAMAICA INN on the Bodmin Moor in Cornwall. A grey slate roof that seems to melt into the cottony clouds of the sky is in some ways a disappointment because it has become so commercial with tourists everywhere. But if you close your eyes and listen carefully, you can still hear the clop-clop of the wreckers' horses on the cobblestoned courtyard as they bring in the loot from ships they lured in to wreck on the rocks near the coast. The seamen on the ships were (accidentally?) drowned, then the looters moved onto the wrecks and took what they wanted. Jamaica Inn was one of the known places where the wreck-

ers' loot was stored. Daphne du Maurier did an outstanding job of bringing these lawless times to life.

There is a small museum of the author's belongings at the inn—a few pages of original hand-penned manuscripts, and many photographs of various honors received at different times in her writing career.

Drop just south of Gweek, then east through Mawgan and on up the road to a hamlet called Kestle (South of the village of Helford on your map. The roads are unnumbered). A footpath leads from Kestle through a deeply-wooded area to FRENCHMAN'S PILL (Cornish word for creek).

This area is exactly like du Maurier described it in the novel. An eerily-lit place—yellow-green from the mist that seems to hang over it day and night—it has a lonely haunted feel, perfect for hiding a colorful pirate ship with sails that snap, flutter, and rise in the breeze to see it to safety in the open sea. One imagines a beautiful young woman gazing through the trees as she waves goodbye to her handsome pirate lover. He waves to her for the last time and tears are wiped away as the curtain falls.

There is a cabin in the area that was once used to hide loot from pirate ships and wreckers.

I spoke to a lady in a Cornwall bookstore about the atmosphere at the creek. She explained that some folks find Frenchman's Creek so eerie, even on a bright summer's day, that they take a look, turn, and scurry quickly up the path without a backward glance.

We hope you'll read *Frenchman's Creek* by du Maurier before you visit Frenchman's Pill. The author grew up on the Lizard Peninsula in Cornwall. It is obvious that she knew her part of the country well.

FRENCHMAN'S CREEK, CORNWALL

TRERICE

Trerice (Ter-rice') is an example of a small (by Britain's standards) country house from which we took some decorating ideas.

This Elizabethan house, built in 1572, lies just outside Newquay on Cornwall's north coast. One of Cornwall's loveliest treasures, it is one of our favorites as well. It is wonderfully livable.

Built of grey stone, it has a broad front with a two-story entrance and beautifully-designed scrolled gables. The interior has a nice collection of seventeenth and eighteenth- century furniture, elaborate plaster ceilings, and a minstrel gallery. Even today a cellist plays from the gallery to entertain guests. (The cellist is only heard, not seen.) We appreciated the idea since we have two professional cellists in our own family who entertain at social gatherings.

The house's most well-known feature is a two-story stone-mullioned window which lights the Great Hall with 576 panes. While the Concorde aircraft was being perfected, it was tested over the coast of Cornwall. Unfortunately the terrific racket and sudden claps of breaking the sound barrier cracked some of the ancient panes in the window and they had to be replaced (because of it the Concorde was rerouted over Wales), but much of the house still retains its sixteenth-century glass. Beneath the window is a wide window seat with a handsome collection of massive blue and white porcelain pieces.

It is not the huge window or the size of the Great Hall that we have adapted to our home, but rather the simple idea of displaying an assortment of blue and white porcelain pieces in a window seat. We already had the collection of blue and white pieces and the window seat. If we had not seen Trerice we probably would still have rather dull house plants spread across the area.

The grounds are planted all around with nice shrubs, climbing roses, and other blooming perennials.

A gigantic stone barn behind the house offers a rustic tea room in one side and in the other one finds what must be the world's largest collection of lawn mowers, tracing their history from the earliest models to some of Britain's latest.

The British are insatiable COLLECTORS. It is common for the houses to have impressive collections of china, glass, or silver, usually family heirlooms. But we enjoy looking for the odd collections in both large and small homes, and some are very odd indeed.

Leeds Castle has a unique collection of *four-hundred-years-worth* of dog collars—leather, bronze, brass, and silver. One house had a collection of motorcycles, from the first rickety device that looked totally unreliable to today's massive models, and surely every model in between. There are collections of ancient wardrobes, artificial limbs for cats, lead soldiers faithfully placed in their actual positions in Napoleonic battles, artificial legs, waxwork figures of royalty in conversational groupings, and one sizable attic housed miniature dollhouse rooms decorated with exquisite miniature period furnishings. There are barns full of chariots and ancient four-wheeled conveyances, medieval weapons and armour, libraries with thousands of books (largely unread, I suspect), vast collections of various types of art, and rooms full of antique musical instruments of all kinds. I guess the one that arrested my attention was the side of one great hall with floor-to-ceiling shelves of sailing ships fashioned from seashells.

CORNISH FISHING VILLAGES

POLRUAN, LOOE, and POLPERRO are but a few of the fishing villages around the coast of Cornwall. They have similar characteristics with minor variations.

The houses are built up the steep cliffsides in layers—a rim of houses, a roadway behind planted along the edges

with shrubbery and flowers. They step up, up, and up in this fashion to the top of the cliff.

It is no wonder photographers love to photograph them and painters have painted them for centuries, for colorful fishing boats with salty captains every bit as captivating, fill these quaint harbors. Sea birds of all kinds reel and scream overhead. While the scene appears lazily stretched out in the sun, most of these villages are working harbors. Local fishermen, looking to bring in a catch each time out, fill the air with salty fresh-fish odors as they unload their catches in flashing pools of writhing silver for local restaurants and markets.

The harbors also offer a great deal of pleasure for those who enjoy water sports.

Some of the villages have incredibly steep, narrow shop-lined streets heading straight downhill to the water. We have yet to get started downhill without having to pass a wide heavily-loaded lory creeping up the hill. We always hope we'll squeeze by it without skinning the lory on one side and a shop front on the other, but a close-up view of the harbor is worth the scare.

It is not at all unusual for cars to drive on the sidewalks on these ancient narrow lanes, so pedestrians beware! Many of the villages have wisely limited all but local traffic. The visitor must park at the top of the village and walk down...and (whew!) climb back out later.

In one of the village parking lots the attendant recognized our car as a rental. He smiled and said, "Oh, we have some Colonials visiting today." We have not only been called Colonials, but many in Britain still refer to us as having come from "The New World."

DWIGHT
WILLIAMS
-NORTH CORNISH COAST-

TINTAGEL

How exciting it is to look over the craggy rocks of the west coast of Cornwall and get a glimpse of the remains of Tintagel Castle, which most folks have learned was the castle seat of King Arthur and his Roundtable. But, sadly, it has been proven that the castle ruins, reached by footpath from the village, have nothing whatever to do with King Arthur and date no earlier than the twelfth century. (King Arthur was sixth century if he existed at all!) The legend was popularized by Tennyson's "The Idylls of the King."

But folklore dies hard, and the truth doesn't prevent the village of Tintagel from promoting the legend as its own. Much of the village's livelihood is dependent on folks who insist that "King Arthur lived in Tintagel castle." Besides a house-turned-shop that sells items dedicated to the king's memory, an interesting Old Post Office works out of a manor house dating from the fourteenth century.

A more realistic interest in this romantic but mysteriously moody spot is in the remains of a much older Celtic monastery, ST. JULIOT, dating from the sixth century. Both it and the Castle once perched high on a ledge over the Atlantic ocean, but crushing waves have washed away the main sections, leaving only sketchy outer walls and foundations.

Three hundred steps reach the site. The first time we were there a storm brought such high winds with fierce slamming waves that it was too risky to take the footpath across the coastal rocks. We found a wind-raked, cloud-enshrouded old church near the coast fascinating and turned our attention to it—wondering why it was built so far from anything else. On a return visit with much nicer weather, the palpable feeling of aloneness on the high cliffs and at the isolated church remained with us.

MORWENSTOW

On the coast north of Tintagel is Morwenstow, famous for its stunning ocean view with some of the highest cliffs in Cornwall. If you have tried to grow sea thrift in your garden you've probably found that it does fairly well with lots of watering. At Morwenstow, as with other places on the Cornish coast, it grows and blooms with wild abandon, carpeting the cliffs in astonishingly brilliant shades of pink.

Fierce Atlantic gales have claimed countless lives of sailors shipwrecked on the rocks below. In a hut overlooking the rocks is where the nineteenth-century eccentric poet and cleric, Robert Stephen Hawker, composed his ballads about the brave men at sea. He spent his time on the cliffs watching for dead sailors to wash up on the shore after a sailing accident, pulled them in, and buried them in the churchyard. His feelings were made known in "Death Song:"

DWIGHT WILLIAMS.
HIGHER SHARPNOSE POINT - Nr. MORWENSTOW,
NORTH CORNISH COAST.

There lies a cold corpse upon the sands
   Down by the rolling sea;
Close up the eyes and straighten the hands,
   As a Christian man's should be....
Lay it among the churchyard stones,
   Where the priest hath blessed the clay;
I cannot leave the unburied bones,
   And I fain would go my way.

OTHER THINGS TO SEE IN THE AREA

WINCHESTER CATHEDRAL was probably first known to most of us from the song by the same name. Spectacular for its size and stone-carved rood screen, it is the longest cathedral in Europe. Built on the foundations of an earlier Saxon structure, the current cathedral was begun in 1079.

SHAFTSBURY is a fascinating medieval town. There is a Saxon cobblestone roadway and part of a Saxon wall on a steep hillside called Gold Hill. You have probably seen it many times in magazine and television advertisements. The quaintness of the cobbled street lined with old houses, each stepping down a full story below its neighbor, and the outstanding view over the countryside while traveling down the steep hill, fills the visitor with awe. The town also has good shopping for daily needs. We had tea in a nostalgic seven-hundred-year-old tea house called King Alfred's Kitchen.

DORCHESTER is a Roman market town founded around AD 70. It was "Casterbridge" in Hardy's novel *The Mayor of Casterbridge.* The town has a great deal of old-world charm. We stayed in the Casterbridge Hotel which served a laudatory table of good English food and was comfortably furnished with all period pieces. Many of the lovely (and grotesque) pieces that furnish inns and country homes are a mixture of periods and styles, some handmade by a family member or a craftsman long forgotten.

HORNINGSHAM, just south of Bradford-on-Avon is a quaint and very pretty village of rolling green hills, scattered farms and thatched cottages, and a Victorian Church dating from 1844. A long and beautiful walk above the village ends at a spot called "Heaven's Gate" where one gets a spectacular view of LONGLEAT HOUSE and grounds below.

Our stay in Horningsham was one of those serendipitous occurrences we hope you, too, will experience. Having changed our plans for a three-day period, we rather casually decided to head in a certain direction, and at an arbitrary point began looking for a bed and breakfast. What we found was one of the nicest homes, owned by some of the nicest people, in one of the nicest villages you can imagine.

South of the village is STOURHEAD GARDENS, planted primarily around a large lake. The garden is of merit for those who enjoy wide forest and parkland with lakes and marble temples. We personally enjoy the more intimate gardens, but this one is rightfully famous.

WESTERN ENGLAND AND THE WELSH BORDER

From Chepstow in southern Wales to the estuary of the River Dee at Chester, England in the north, is the area called the Marches. The name refers to a district set up to defend a common boundary—in this case the Welsh-English border country. It is no wonder it has many interesting small castles and fortified houses, even fortified churches, where brave souls stood their ground. Early it was the Romans versus the Celts, then the Saxons versus the Welsh, later the Roundheads versus the Royalists in the Civil War. The powerful neighbor, England, versus the small stubborn neighbor, Wales—it has never been an easy border.

THE BLACK MOUNTAINS

Along some eighty square miles of the Welsh Border, starting at Abergavenny in the south and ending at Hay-on-Wye in the north, sprawl the Black Mountains—three ragged ridges covered with bracken. The area is hauntingly wild and sparsely populated. There are still mysterious Welsh tales of inexplicable suicides, incest, and whispers of witchcraft.

The mountains lived up to their rather dreary reputation the murky, fog-enshrouded day we drove through them in a downpour. As we drove along we thought about how the Welsh had hidden among the ridges from the Normans. The residents still carry hangover anger at England, the causes long-since forgotten. We were reminded of it when we heard a woman who worked at Heathrow Airport exclaim to another, "Don't call me a bloody Englishman. I'm from Wales!"

To add to the disconcerting silence of the area, we passed the skeleton of Llanthony Abbey atop the ridges, sending its dark spikes and romantic arches jutting eerily into the sky. The spot was so austere and remote that the Augustinian group had difficulty keeping members, who insisted on gravitating down the mountain to a more friendly environment. Wales can, indeed, be mysterious, even baleful.

KILPECK CHURCH AND ABBEY DORE

You'll never see a more beautiful little church in Britain than the Church of St. Mary and St. David at Kilpeck. The south door is considered one of the finest examples of stone

DETAIL KILPECK CHURCH

carving anywhere. A mixture of motifs—flowers, fruits, serpents, dragons, and warriors are intertwined in a writhing mass of pink stone. The full meaning of the carvings has never been deciphered. The particular style cannot be seen anywhere else in Britain as it was done by Spanish carvers brought in especially for that particular job.

A frieze running around the eaves of the church has carved corbels depicting human and animal heads. The church has been virtually unchanged since the eleven hundreds.

We enjoyed the churchyard as much as the building. The flowers, trees, and lawns are a perfect foil for ancient scaly gravestones.

The original part of ABBEY DORE was built at the end of the twelfth century. Only the transepts, crossing, and chancel remain today with a seventeenth-century tower and wall paintings.

It is the small things you happen onto that make an investigation of abbey ruins worthwhile, and we were not to be disappointed at Abbey Dore. Fragments of sculpture from the oldest parts of the abbey were saved, including effigies of two cross-legged knights from the thirteenth century, and a collection of well-preserved tiles from the same era.

Both the abbey and the Kilpeck Church are in the Golden Valley along or near the River Dore, one of the most quietly beautiful sections of all England.

THE BLACK AND WHITE TRAIL

The River Wye and the River Arrow tend to bracket a peaceful area. West of Leominster (Lem'-ster), a series of small medieval villages are built in the black and white style typical of the Marches, the buildings spanning a thousand years of history. They are included in an auto tour the locals call The Black and White Trail. The villages are arranged in a circuit and include Kington, Lyonshall, Pembridge, Eardisland, Dilwyn, Weobley, Sarnesfield, Kinnerseley, and Eardisley. Scattered between and around them are other smaller villages and hamlets with their share of interesting medieval architecture.

It is important to note that these houses have not always been painted black and white. Originally the oak timbers were left to weather a comfortable pearly grey. Black and white was a Victorian idea.

We visited most of these villages and found them fascinating, but some we remember with special fondness.

PEMBRIDGE is a favorite, not only for black and white houses, but for an enticing little gift shop called "Junk and Disorderly." We have spent some happy afternoons sorting through antiques, handmade gifts, and other unusual items, bringing back a few small things to enjoy in our own home.

The Old Chapel Gallery in Pembridge has a collection of contemporary sculpture—handmade furniture, rugs, paintings, and other arts and crafts. Central in the village is The New Inn which seems misnamed to western Americans since the graceful structure is over six hundred years old.

We enjoy EARDISLAND for its tidy beauty. The River Arrow meanders through the village with a maze of colorful little gardens and black and white, and sometimes brick homes along both sides. An unusually tall brick dovecote

catches a photographer's eye. The two-arch bridge over the river completes a picture of serenity.

Dwight dubs DILWYN "the nicest village to live in." It's off the main road and has a cheerful but quiet look about it that grabs his attention. He says it is even less well known than the other villages and therefore quieter.

WEOBLEY will always remain a favorite for its Olde Salutation Inn, a pub with exceptionally fine food. We have been there enough times to become acquainted with the establishment and its ways, which makes it even more fun to go back time and again. The lamb with rosemary sauce is unforgettable.

SARNESFIELD has a well-kept stone church that dates from the twelfth century. We find that churches built that early often have the most extraordinary furnishings, including the original ancient trunks that still hold old church documents. Sarnesfield has fragments of some of the earliest stained glass enhancing its windows, and on the top of the west tower is one of the most handsome gold cock weather vanes anywhere.

ROSE COTTAGE

We stumbled onto an Elizabethan half-timber in the hamlet of Woonton in the black and white area. The house is called Rose Cottage and is our idea of the best bed and breakfast in Britain—a favorite destination when we are in the Marches.

It is a pleasant combination of a timbered house and gardens lovingly kept by an accommodating and friendly hostess. While caring for a family, she is still able to give endless attention to detail for the comfort of her guests with no apparent stress on her part. Tea at a rustic table in her garden of vintage roses and herbs is a pleasure to remember.

The house is primarily Victorian inside with her plants, collections, books, and desk near at hand. Our bedroom was outfitted with all white sheets, comforter, lacy pillows and dust ruffle—an intimate spot for a good night's sleep.

One evening her young son asked Dwight if he would help him draw his mother's garden. Dwight happily obliged. The boy and his mother were pleased with the results.

From across a meadow near Rose Cottage we can hear cuckoos calling. Folks who live nearby claim the sound is a nuisance, but since we never hear them any other time we enjoy waking up to their toy-like calls.

In our collective memory of favorite areas in all of Britain, always at or near the top is this part of Herefordshire, west of Leominster and along the Welsh border.

LUDLOW

Ludlow was begun in the twelfth century around a Norman border castle. The castle is in ruins, but the round Norman Chapel and some of the state rooms are still intact. During the time of the Tudors and the Stuarts it was the headquarters for the Council of the Marches established to administer the wild Welsh border country.

The town has many fine old buildings and the largest parish church in England.

One notable building is an elaborate black and white half-timbered inn, The Feathers Hotel. It has carved panelling and fifteenth-century wall paintings plus an exemplary reputation for good food. A geological museum may be of interest to some visitors.

Ludlow and the nearby Clun valley are central to the poetic writings of A. E. Housman.

STOKESAY CASTLE

Actually a moated fortified manor house, the name Stokesay means "the dairy farm (Stoke) of the Say family." It is interesting from an architectural standpoint. The visitor enters through a seventeenth-century timber-framed gatehouse (painted a sunny yellow) and finds himself in a walled courtyard with colorful flowers, plants, and foliage spilling from every nook and cranny.

The architecture of the English house took form over several centuries, and Stokesay is a good example. The house, started in the thirteenth century, consists of a Great Hall with two towers, one at either end. In its medieval days a collection of separate wooden buildings filled the area between the

towers. A century later the buildings were replaced with stone structures pulled together by the Great Hall in the center with rooms splaying out from it for family privacy.

A withdrawing room to which the ladies could retire from the drinking and revelry of the Great Hall, was probably the beginning of the English house as we know it. It was a welcome place for ladies to rest and pamper themselves in privacy.

Entering the vast Great Hall now empty of furnishings, one realizes how complicated the roof structure is and how ingenious early carpenters tied the whole of the huge room together with cruck timbers (oak timbers chosen by shape to fit the shape of the roof).

An interesting aspect of Stokesay is the three-story five-sided North Tower with its projecting timber work. It gives the building a somewhat rustic appearance. From the outside, the whole of the castle has the look of an ancient ship rising above the moat.

Across the moat is the village church. It s yard, blooming with knots of snowy Queen Anne's Lace, lends a timeless grace to the ancient and weathered gravestones.

DWIGHT WILLIAMS
~CHURCH OF ST. GEORGE
CLUN, SHROPSHIRE~

CLUN

We first became acquainted with the Marches because we read about the Clun Church having a "double pyramid roof." What did that mean? Of course we had to find out.

The Clun Valley is a peaceful spot today, but the border village of Clun grew up around its castle despite both Saxon and Welsh attacks during the Middle Ages. Later, harassment came from both the Roundheads and the Royalists during the Civil War. The village was forced to organize to fight off both sides.

A medieval saddleback bridge over the River Clun takes travelers from one side of the village, where dramatic castle ruins anchor the hillside, to St. George's Church. Watching over the village from its perch on the opposite hill, St. George's is believed to occupy the site of a Druidic Seminary. The old church tower, stepping up to two roof levels (that double pyramid), has a fortress look all its own. An attractive lychgate at the end of the church walk gives a wide view over village and countryside.

There are four villages in the valley with Clun in their name; Clunton, Clunbury, Clungunford and Clun. A. E. Housman called them the "quietest places under the Sun" in *A Shropshire Lad.*

After some rather healthy climbs up and down steep hills all afternoon we threw our low-fat diet to the wind and satisfied ourselves with tea and a scrumptious piece of orange cake in a delightful little tearoom furnished with antiques. We've been back several times.

WENLOCK PRIORY

SHREWSBURY

Shrewsbury was a fortress town protected by a horseshoe bend in the River Severn and a twelfth-century castle. Bridges across the river leave no doubt that its soldiers played a major part in marching back and forth in border skirmishes.

Shrewsbury is still a busy market center with markets three days a week. There is a museum of local history and archaeology and another of fine Coalport China made in the area in the eighteenth century. The church of St. Mary's contains a famous fourteenth-century Jesse window.

Charles Darwin, author of *The Origin of Species* and *Descent of Man,* was born and raised in Shrewsbury. Shrewsbury Abbey is also the home of mystery fiction's Brother Cadfael, made famous in the writings of Ellis Peters and a series on PBS television.

WENLOCK PRIORY, IRON BRIDGE, AND WIGHTWICK are not exactly in The Marches, but they are worth a detour to the east.

WENLOCK PRIORY

Just southeast of Shrewsbury at Much Wenlock are the fascinating remains of Wenlock Priory. It was founded about 680, destroyed by the Danes two hundred years later, then refounded by Cluniac monks in 1050.

When we arrived we were given earphones and a tape of "an early monk" guiding us through extensive remains of the abbey and telling us, in first person, about the life of solitude within its cloistered walls. The organization's demise came about by the same route many others do—greed, selfishness, competition, too much wealth—all things from which abbey life was supposed to be free. As with most abbey ruins, the grounds are so well kept you feel like you're in a beautiful park.

DWIGHT
WILLIAMS
—IRONBRIDGE—

IRON BRIDGE

For those who have an interest in feats of mechanical and structural engineering, the world's first iron bridge, cast in the nearby COALBROOKDALE Company ironworks of Abraham Darby, should not be overlooked. The bridge is located in the village of Iron Bridge just east of the Marches.

Neither bolts nor rivets had been invented when this arched bridge was built over the River Severn in 1779. Instead, the bridge was put together with wood joinery shapes cast in iron. Modern experts claim the bridge was overbuilt by several times, weighing in at a massive 378 tons.

The bridge is no longer open to traffic, but a hike along the riverbank below brings you close enough to inspect the bridge's unique construction and take close-up photographs.

Abraham Darby was the early ironmaster at the Coalbrookdale Company. He used coke rather than charcoal to fuel his furnaces, which made iron less expensive and quicker to produce. The innovation was a primary factor in the Industrial Revolution. A museum in Coalbrookdale tells the story of its beginnings. Relics of this great movement in history can be seen throughout the area.

DWIGHT
WILLIAMS.

LITTLE MORETON HALL,
CHESHIRE

LITTLE MORETON HALL

Before we leave the border country, although slightly outside of it, we would like to call attention to three outstanding houses.

Little Moreton Hall, a moated and totally picturesque house started in 1250, may be the best known timber-framed house in England. It certainly is one of the most elaborate with timbered decoration everywhere. Someone once called it "a vast unstable doll's house," which seems fairly accurate when one gazes at it and can't find a single segment that looks plumb.

The Great Hall was "modernized" in 1599 and has not been remodeled since. Early panelling, painted tile ceilings, and several decorated fireplaces carry through the medieval style.

The house is empty of furnishings except for chests in the hall and a great round table in the parlor.

We enjoyed exploring the many facets of Little Moreton Hall and pondered the idea that anyone would go to such fanciful extremes in building a private home.

WIGHTWICK

To the east of Shrewsbury near Wolverhampton is Wightwick Manor. A half-timbered manor house built in 1887, it stands in many ways as a revolt against the Industrial Revolution.

The artistic movement displayed so elegantly here was established, at least in part, as a protest to early days of modern mass-production. William Morris, John Ruskin, Sir Edward Burne-Jones, Dante Gabriel and Christina Rossetti, plus other Pre-Raphaelite artists, used Wightwick to show their collected works of fabric designs, wallpapers, tiles, stained glass, watercolors, and other artistic endeavours. And what a splendid show it is!

The house is decorated outside with spiral Tudor chimneys and intricate wood carving. Some of the black-and-white designs were patterned after Little Moreton Hall, the famous half-timber you read about above. The wood carving is carried through the interior, lending a special warmth to the surroundings. The gardens are formal with topiary, roses, and wide expanses of lawn.

We were so impressed with Wightwick that our own new home is designed around Dwight's studio along lines that use some of Wightwick's characteristics. Our home is not as large or elaborate, of course, but it does have an English flavor. The house is full of Dwight's paintings, many pieces of furniture he has designed and built himself, as well as my own needlework, photographs, and interior decorating. The feel is warm and personal—easy to live with.

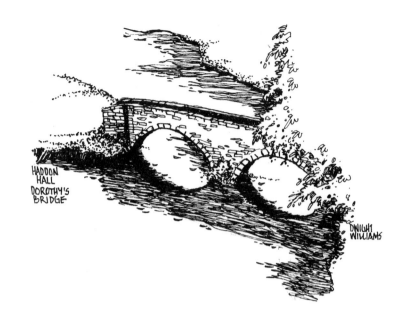

HADDON
HALL
DOROTHY'S
BRIDGE

DWIGHT
WILLIAMS

HADDON HALL

Haddon Hall, southwest of Sheffield near Bakewell, is an extremely well preserved medieval home above the River Wye (a different River Wye). Built around a courtyard, it seems oddly plain, yet regal, beneath its starkly crenelated towers and turrets—the oldest parts dating to the twelfth century. The house was lived in until the eighteenth century, then left abandoned for nearly two hundred years. In the twentieth century, restoration was undertaken with the same materials from which it was originally built.

The Great Hall is rather stark. Animal racks and skins as the only wall decoration lend it a hunting lodge personality. A long heavy oak table in the center of the hall is testimony to the feasts enjoyed there after hunting parties.

Large bay windows in the long gallery are known for having a few of the leaded lights bulge outward to reflect light from several angles. Catching the blue of the sky or the green of the gardens, the clear lights appear to be a range of colors.

The chapel contains medieval wallpaintings and a sensitive marble sculpture of a male child who had met an untimely death. When the visitor learns that the piece was sculpted by his mother early in the twentieth century, it becomes even more poignant.

Freshly-cut flowers have been an important ingredient in English homes for centuries, along with pleasantly-scented herb gardens for use in the kitchen. The herbs impart touches of green to the lush floral beds as well. At Haddon Hall these stately mixed terrace gardens dazzle the eye with brilliant color throughout the summer.

Below the terraces a picturesque stone-arched bridge crosses the river. There, it is said, Dorothy Vernon, daughter of the household in the sixteenth century, ran away from a family party, crossed the bridge in the dark of night, and eloped with her lover, John Manners. The house has belonged to the Manners family ever since.

BOSWORTH FIELD

Slightly west of Leicester, and a few miles north of Coventry, is Bosworth Field Battleground. The pastoral scene today masks the bloody battle of 1485 when Henry Tudor defeated the last Plantagenet King, Richard III, to begin a new royal lineage. The battle, culminating in the king's death, effectively ended the political intrigue and underhanded dealings that came to be known as the Wars of The Roses.

Well-documented signboards mark the spots where forces on both sides (as many as twenty thousand men) prepared for battle. Standards with large heraldic flags mark the likely spots where the battle leaders stood. A visitor's center brings the battle to life with model knights, archers, and foot soldiers.

The king was said to have prayed at the SUTTON CHENEY VILLAGE CHURCH nearby just prior to the battle. Apparently it didn't help.

OTHER THINGS TO SEE

The Marches is a splendid area to spend an extra day turning off on side roads—enjoying beautiful HOMES AND GARDENS in hamlets and villages. As you get into the country there are nice stone barns and lovely old parish churches to explore.

WEIR GARDENS - an outstanding garden of specimen trees, shrubs, and parkland built on a very steep side of the River Wye.

PERSHORE ABBEY - an exceptionally beautiful Benedictine house with a very elegant interior. It is a building of interesting shape because it uses the remains (the crossing, choir and south transept) of what was once a much larger abbey church. The choir limb has been used as a parish church for centuries, thus escaping demolition in the dissolution.

WALES

When we first drove into Wales we were not quite sure what to expect. We had read about the mysterious quality of the mist-swept countryside, its background of strange Celtic people with their bent for folk music, unique poetry, curious superstitions, and ghoulish Druids.

What we found was a land of intense and variegated shades of green—land that rolls in humps and swales—rocky hills, deep valleys, mountains, lakes, and grand vistas that often open unexpectedly to the sea. Moody clouds gliding in on ocean breezes sometimes keep a light drizzle going for days, while unconcerned sheep and cattle graze the meadows in the most pastoral of scenes.

But there is another side to Wales. Sections of the north, moving out toward the Island of Anglesey, are still bleak and depressed from early slate quarries, and the scars of coal mining in the south are not entirely gone either. A myriad of castles dot the hillsides in all directions—some six hundred have been counted and named over the centuries—many in ruins or no longer in existence. The fact that Edward I had to build so many gigantic fortresses in the eight-thousand-square-mile area to squelch their independence makes it obvious that the Welsh did not accept lightly the idea of being conquered by the English. The seat of power is in London, and has been for seven hundred years, but the small country has not lost its will to maintain its Celtic heritage.

Its people call Wales Cymru (kim'-roo), forging a bond amongst themselves with a revival of the Welsh language. They proclaim in a determined way that those who do not speak Welsh are not Welsh and therefore cannot perpetuate the ancient communal memories that are so important to the survival of a lost Celtic civilization. Some historians claim that it was from the ashes of this communal memory, the heroes growing ever more heroic as the centuries passed, that the legend of King Arthur arose.

So what does one finally make of Wales? Acceptance. Accept it for what it is and enjoy the fact that it is different.

WELSH DRAGON

CHEPSTOW CASTLE

Our breath was caught in awe at sight of our first medieval military castle, sprawled along a ridge above the River Wye like a resting but wary cat spreads her long agile body across a tree branch. A forty-foot-high keep and ominous twin towers rose mightily into the air.

Cold grey stone walls and deepening shadows within the immense roofless caverns kept us gawking and silently imagining what life must have been like within the castle so many centuries ago when guardsmen had to be posted on the highest ramparts to protect those inside.

We spent most of the afternoon wandering from one section of the fort to another, peeping through narrow slits straight down sheer stone walls into the river that had once served as a natural moat for the castle.

We were pleased to discover Chepstow first because it is one of the oldest castles built of stone in Britain, possibly in all of Europe. It was started in 1068 with outer defensive walls added in the thirteenth century.

When we had satisfied ourselves that we had seen it all (and having taken far more photographs of the castle than anyone could ever possibly need), we left to look over the town.

The PORT OF CHEPSTOW was once a thriving center for trade with Europe. Some steep streets on the cliffside are still cobbled. Glass-engraving is demonstrated in the old schoolhouse which is now known as the Stuart Crystal Center.

THE CASTLES OF EDWARD I

Chepstow is the barest beginning of the castles to see in Wales. In 1283, King Edward I of England began building a series of fortresses and towns in strategic locations throughout Wales. These were meant to be used for the conquest of Wales, but the castles and walls around the towns built at their base were primarily defensive structures.

The castles were built on a hill or large outcropping of rock near a river or seaside, and were meant to protect the town built around it. The water was used to enclose the castle with a wide moat. Generally an outer stone wall called a curtain wall was built with another wall inside it for even more protection.

Unlike many castles in other parts of Britain, Wales's military castles were never turned into private homes. It is amazing how extensive the remains are (the stone was not taken to build other buildings in the area) after the passing of so many centuries.

For those who care to pursue the details of medieval castle-building, there are a number of books available on the subject. A traveler might want to know more about it if castle-touring sparks his interest. Let me introduce you to three of Edward's most interesting castle remains.

CAERNARFON Castle looms over the southern end of the Menai Strait and is considered one of the greatest examples of military architecture. Edward I used it as an administrative center for the Northern part of the country.

Thirteen towers rise above the twenty-foot-thick walls, all differing in size and design, the foundations under them cut from solid stone. A town was settled near its base from which a wall went out for protection.

In the thirteenth century, Edward's wife gave birth at Caernarfon to the Prince Edward who became the first English Prince of Wales, a title now hereditary to the sovereign's eldest son. The first investiture of a Prince of Wales, heir to the British throne, took place at Caernarfon in 1911. Today the castle is probably best known for the investiture of the current Prince Charles as the Prince of Wales in 1969.

The town has a museum devoted to its sea faring history, and another detailing an early Celtic community of dwellings, shops, and taverns.

HARLECH is one of the smaller fortresses of Edward I built to subdue the Welsh. The castle sets squarely on top of a rocky hill two hundred feet above the sea and was meant to appear overwhelming and frightening. In times past the sea surrounded the base of the rock, but it has receded some distance from it now.

Years of violence between the English and the Welsh shook the castle. It was once under siege for seven years during The Wars of the Roses. Its active history came to an end during the English Civil War, for it was the last Royalist stronghold in Wales.

The castle was self-contained with its own well. Inside its high remaining walls are a chapel, a bakery, and a great hall with its buttery (an ale cellar), pantry and kitchen.

49

Started in 1295, BEAUMARIS Castle was the only defense Edward I had on Anglesey and the last of his Welsh castles to be built. It had an elaborate system of defenses which were never put to the test, for the castle was never completed.

After thirty-five years of work, rotting timbers and a good deal of three shades of red stonework showed deterioration. Yet much of it remains intact.

Today the town of Beaumaris is a holiday resort and sailing center with a pleasant mixture of well-preserved buildings dating from the medieval period. The beauty of the location on the Menai strait looking across to Snowdonia is a spectacular sight.

OTHER THINGS TO SEE ON ANGLESEY

The rest of the Island of Angelsey has sights worth seeing. Just to the southwest of Beaumaris is PLAS NEWYDD, an impressive sixteenth-century house with many Rex Whistler paintings, including a large detailed mural, and a lovely spring garden graced with azaleas and rhododendrons.

PENMON PRIORY, Augustinian, is an isolated area on the eastern-most point of Anglesey. It has romantic ruins, part of which are used as a parish church.

Following the coast around Red Wharf Bay to the north, the village of MOELFRE provides an interesting walk on an oceanside path where the views to sea are spectacular and an isolated shed houses the life-saver's boat that goes out on SOS in the bay. Fishing villages and other coastal areas often have such volunteer rescue organizations. The rescue boats are treated like an ambulance service. They are cleaned thoroughly everyday by the volunteers who man them, and all working parts are checked and made ready for sudden departure.

The boat at Moelfre had been out the night before we saw it to rescue a group of careless teenagers who had gone out on the bay against poor weather predictions. The keeper at the boathouse was visibly annoyed about the stunt, and who can blame him? There are many monuments and sad tales of fishermen and others lost in treacherous waters all along the coasts of Britain.

Just west of Moelfre is DIN LLIGWY, dramatic ruins of a stone fort the Celts used to hide from the Romans in the fourth century.

TALYLLLYN RAILWAY

Wales and the rest of Britain have a number of restored old-time railways. Talyllyn on the Welsh west coast is a narrow-gauge line constructed in 1865 to carry slate from a quarry above Abergynolwyn (you're on your own pronouncing this one) to be moved to its destination by coastal rail.

Passengers board the train at Abergynolwyn station and enjoy a scenery-filled ride to the Tywyn station and back, a round trip of about fourteen miles in an open railcar. Tywyn's terminal houses a Narrow Gauge Railway Museum. There is plenty of time to look it over and have a snack before starting back.

We felt like kids again the sunny afternoon we were whisked through wild wooded areas, colorful rocky canyons, and an occasional isolated hamlet—all places we would not have seen otherwise. It was a pleasant change to sit back, relax, and let someone else do the driving.

We have not ridden other Welsh railways, but we did ride the BLUE BELL RAILWAY in Southern England and enjoyed the trip with other friendly railway buffs. The Blue Bell, a standard-gauge line, owns and operates one of Britain's largest collections of old railway equipment. We suspect any of the restored railways marked on your map in any part of Britain would be an enjoyable ride.

POWIS CASTLE AND GARDENS

There are many unusual and beautiful things to see at Powis (Po'-is). The house, built of rich sandstone, has a confident air as it overlooks the Severn Valley. Walls and crenelated towers rise above stone terraces with climbers and ingenious plantings woven in and around each other with such grace you feel as though you're in a delicate hanging garden.

Trimmed yew hedges are punctuated with lead statuary, shrubs, masses of colorful flowers, and an occasional peacock that strolls the grounds, only to give out a bloodcurdling scream for "help" when attention lags.

Wavy-patterned yew topiary flows over walls and stair balustrades like a spontaneous emerald-green waterfall. A wooded area contains fine specimen trees.

The fortified castle was built around 1200 and gradually changed character through the centuries to become a lovely and unique palace. Portraits by old masters ornament the walls. French and English furnishings, accented with an occasional inlaid Italian piece, distinguish the house's interior. The Clive Museum (Clive is a family name) holds a collection of East Indian works of art.

On a hill across from the house and above the gardens we were delighted to see a sweep of parkland dedicated to a collection of modern sculpture, their undefined shapes in sharp contrast to the eighteenth-century pieces near the house.

ERDDIG

Historians claim that the unusual thing about Erddig (Er'-thig) is that the owners never threw anything away. The house is a fascinating clutter of catchalls and collections kept since the rather plain, but mammoth red brick house was built in the 1680s. If you were a fan of the PBS show *Upstairs, Downstairs,* you'll enjoy a journey through rooms that seem familiar.

The visitor enters through the workyard where the out-buildings and below-stairs servants' workrooms have their original fittings. From these areas you can see that Erddig was a self-contained community. There are stables, a black-smith shop, bakehouse, sawmill, a laundry, and other facilities once operated exclusively by the servants. After a day's exhausting work they climbed the steep back stairs to their attic bedrooms, rooms still laid out today just as they were in the eighteenth and nineteenth centuries.

The family (The Yorkes) committed their servants to a place in history in a series of individual photographs, labeled by name and period of service. The collection hangs in the servants' hall.

The house retains much of its original parkland-style landscaping and furniture. Among the most important pieces is a state bed with Chinese embroidered hangings.

BODNANT GARDENS

Bodnant Gardens sets high over the River Conwy in northern Wales with a grand view of Snowdonia. We had read about the gardens numerous times but had paid little attention. When we were in the area talking to bed and breakfast hosts, folks in pubs, various conversations in shops and on the street, we heard the same remark: "Oh, please, don't leave Wales without seeing the Laburnum Walk at Bodnant Gardens." One excited lady added, "It's (the Laburnum) in full bloom right now. You simply mustn't miss it!"

Could any garden be that special? The only answer I can give is...well...Don't leave Wales without seeing the Laburnum walk at Bodnant Gardens!

An avenue of pleached blooming Laburnums (we know Laburnum as the Golden Chain Tree) washes the arched area with a vibrant sunny glow as it leads the visitor through a wild garden and onto a lawn planted with specimen trees.

A handsome black and white half-timbered house dominates the hilltop as it towers over the breathtaking five-terraced garden. The high stone walls and stairways of the terraces are banked with rock cress, roses, camellias, hydrangeas, and other ornamental shrubs, providing an astonishing range of color and design. We were taken by the beauty of handmade wooden finials that topped off the arbors at regular intervals.

Formal lily ponds and an extensive rose garden complete a more formal area.

There is something about a beautiful garden that makes us smile as it unleashes a mood of hope and satisfaction in our lives. Bodnant is, indeed, a special place. It even produced some prize-winning photographs for me at our Western Idaho fair.

ST. DAVID'S CATHEDRAL

For safety's sake, you'll find St. David's Cathedral tucked in a natural hollow out of the sight of nosy sea raiders. A monastic group had been founded on the same spot in the sixth century by St David, Patron Saint of Wales, after whom the city and cathedral are named.

The Cathedral is built from an unusual purple-grey sandstone taken from local quarries. A native Irish oak nave roof is noteworthy. Medieval architecture throughout makes a tour worthwhile.

There are ruins of an opulent Bishop's Palace nearby which suggests that the thirteenth-century Cathedral enjoyed great wealth.

PEMBROKE CASTLE

Many fascinating castles with extensive remains in Wales have nothing to do with Edward I. Pembroke is one of them. The most memorable things about Pembroke are its mighty round eighty-foot-high keep, and that it was the birthplace of Henry Tudor in 1457, the winner of the battle at Bosworth Field you read about above. He was the first of the powerful Tudor dynasty, father of Henry VIII, and grandfather of Elizabeth I.

As you come upon it, the walls of the castle, ringed solemnly with lookout towers, give a stern warning-away look. In the blunt round keep a circular staircase cut into its wall leads to the top and an outstanding view of the countryside.

MANORBIER CASTLE

This is a small minor castle on the south coast, a nobleman's seat, started in the twelfth century. Interesting mostly from an architectural standpoint, the castle contains a stone-built hall block that rises two exceedingly-high stories. History suggests that after its prime it was a nicely secluded spot for smugglers to hide their loot.

Our interest in it is the way the castle perches on the hillside. Its sheer high walls drop dramatically into a Queen Anne's Lace-dappled hole, suggesting that the structure is far more formidable than it actually is. The hall is occupied, but many of the outer buildings have fallen to ruins.

We always explore ruins. It gives you a chance to see how a structure was built. We're always amazed at the thickness of castle walls, for instance, and puzzle over how workmen got such large heavy stones in place high into the air.

There is an attractive flower garden inside Manorbier's gate.

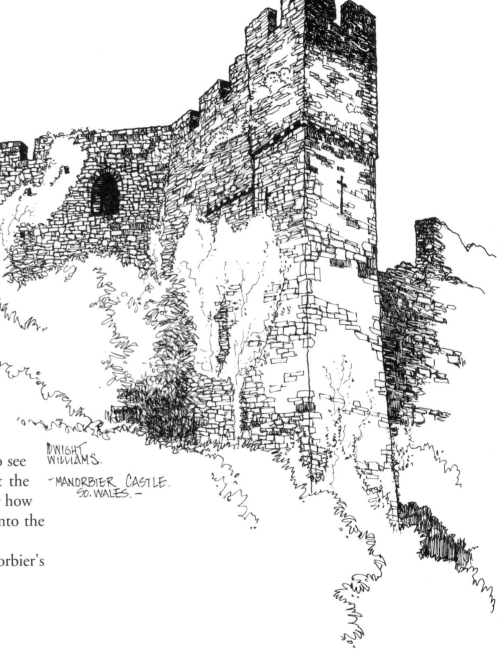

DWIGHT WILLIAMS.
-MANORBIER CASTLE. SO. WALES. -

DWIGHT
WILLIAMS
- NORTH WALES -

OTHER THINGS TO SEE

We suggest a drive down the LLEYN PENINSULA to see PLAS-YN-RHIW, a tenth-century National Trust house near the ocean with a subtropical garden, as well as other sights on the way.

TREGARON is a very Welsh town (they speak only Welsh to each other) leading to ABERGWESYN PASS, often referred to as "The Great Welsh Desert." The unnumbered road runs between Tragaron and Beulah. It rises and falls with the largely uninhabited upland country where the views carry on in endless patterns under skies mottled with cottonball clouds. A short hairpin-bend called DEVIL'S STAIRCASE plunges steeply downhill. It seems to frighten Welsh drivers. Any Idahoan who remembers the old White Bird Hill will be amused.

Watch your map for WOOLLEN MILLS spotted here and there. You can watch them weave wool cloth and at some you can buy stylish sweaters and other woollens at fair prices.

Wool is still an important industry in Wales. We enjoyed staying in a bed and breakfast where the host was a Border Collie trainer. The dogs are essential to the sheep growers and become part of the family. It is interesting to watch the shepherd control them with a few whistles and hand motions, but we were more fascinated with how the dogs seem to help train each other, the older ones taking charge of the younger and, with a nip here and there, making sure they do their share and do it properly.

DRIVES - Wales is a beautiful country from one end to the other. Any drive you might take will be rewarding. A particularly nice one is in the Clwydian range at the North end of Offa's dike (earthworks built by the Mercian King, Offa, to separate his land from Wales) above a village called Bodfari. Not far away, take unmarked roads above GLYN CEIRIOG just south of Llangollen, or around BALA LAKE and LAKE VYRNWY.

As you travel backroads you'll happen onto castle ruins in many of the villages. While they may be too obscure to be listed on your map, the sites are almost always signposted. We find them irresistible and have to stop to see what took place there and snap a photograph for future reference.

We recommend a drive through the northern SNOW-DONIA country where heavy clouds of mist often blanket the mountain tops. If you arrive on a sunny day you are an extremely lucky person and blessed with spectacular scenery.

Wales may be one of the best places of all to just strike out and make your own discoveries. The whole of the Welsh coast is beautiful and a playground for water sports.

ABERYSTWYTH is a university town with pastel-painted Victorian buildings and a glorious view of Cardigan Bay.

DWIGHT
WILLIAMS.
—THE GUILDHALL of
CORPUS CHRISTI.
LAVENHAM, SUFFOLK—

EAST ANGLIA

A good deal of East Anglia can be seen even if time is short. North of London, East Anglia consists of the counties of Essex, Suffolk, Norfolk, and parts of Cambridgeshire and Lincolnshire. It is not a precise geographic region. In our opinion the swamp-drained fens and flat farmland of the area are not as geographically interesting as the rolling green hills and rugged moors and dales of other parts of Britain. But there are special places here too.

LAVENHAM

Lavenham was a wool town in its early days, dating mostly from the fifteenth century. Today, there are still many weavers' stone cottages that intermingle with merchants' half-timber houses along the streets. Visitors have a feeling they're not getting a square look at the world when they see how the town houses have settled against each other in crooked and restless-looking slouches—most of them drenched in pale pink. "Suffolk Pink" is traditionally a mixture of oxblood, bull urine, lime, and water, a predominant color on structures not only in Lavenham, but throughout Suffolk. It is a centuries-old formula used to preserve the mud-plastered exteriors of timber-built buildings.

The folks who live in Lavenham publicize the town as "the finest medieval town in England with superb ancient buildings." Over three hundred of these buildings along the original medieval street patterns are listed as being of architectural and historic importance.

There is an exceptionally fine Guildhall built in 1529. The early guilds were formed to meet the mutual interests of those involved in the wool trade. The hall contains exhibits that explain how the clothiers prospered in East Anglia before the Industrial Revolution, how wool was carded with teasel, and various samples of weaving styles. Blue wool broadcloth and horsehair crinoline were the town specialties.

The stone and flint tower of St. Peter and St. Paul looks over the town from the brow of the hill.

If you want to visit a town that will satisfy your storybook longings of "a typical English village," then do see Lavenham.

When we began thinking about building our own new home, Dwight took our plans to a builder and showed him pictures of several crooked houses in Lavenham simply as an example of the style we were considering. The builder took one look at the skewed structures, winked at his partner, and said, "I think we'd better let our competition build this one."

GIFFORD'S HALL

Gifford's Hall is a timber-framed and moated manor house built in 1480. It was a time in East Anglia when the wealthy searched for new ways to show off their gains. Placing vertical timbers close together on the exterior, then infilling with plaster, became the style. On some of the houses the whole was then covered with plaster and pargeted (elegant raised designs made in wet plaster).

One of the striking things about Gifford's Hall is that part of the exterior was plastered over and pargeted, while part was left with the vertical timbers exposed, allowing them to weather to a soft natural grey. An interesting pattern of brick infill decorates the siding around the entrance. Handsome high brick chimneys grab your attention from some distance.

The house settles nicely into a lush garden of blooming roses and rhododendrons near the foundations, while across the moat, hedges, oval arbors, and decorative fences with fancifully-carved animals on the posts, divide the gardens into more formal areas. When we arrived a gardener was carefully preparing the place for a rare open-house weekend.

DWIGHT WILLIAMS
-Trimming the boxwood-
GIFFORD'S HALL, WICKHAMBROOK, SUFFOLK.

We were sorry we were not allowed inside the house to see a splendid plaster ceiling we had read about. How the big houses are arranged and furnished is always of interest to us. I suspect Gifford's Hall might well be filled with a treasure of original things. The gardener told us that a lady lives alone in the big house (she's elderly now), and has for many years.

DWIGHT
WILLIAMS -

CASTLE
RISING.

CASTLE RISING

While preparing for trips to Britain, we had several times read with interest about Castle Rising. We had studied an aerial view that made it look irresistible, but had never had a chance to get there. When we finally saw it we were sorry we had not gone sooner. I can't think of a better place to gain an understanding of what earthwork defenses were all about and why they were used so extensively.

The earthworks around Castle Rising are considered spectacular examples of well-preserved Norman fortifications.

The castle is surrounded by an earth rampart sixty-four feet high. An outer moat, which surrounds the rampart, drops another sixty feet below its base. A sturdy bridge crosses the moat to a large grassy area inside the earthworks where the castle sets—not an easy place for ground troops to break into.

In 1183, the squat square keep was built. The magnificence of the rooms was meant to convey the owner's wealth. One can easily imagine how impressive it might have been, even though the wooden floors and roof are long gone, leaving only the stone walls.

The forebuilding has survived nearly intact. It has a startlingly beautiful stone staircase with interlacing arches leading into it. Glancing up that long sweep of irregular moss-tinted steps with intermittent fancifully-carved corbels on the arches, was one of the times we stopped suddenly and found our mouths hanging open in awe.

Other castle buildings are the remains of a Norman church, built before the keep, and a Norman gatehouse with a room above the entrance passage.

With all of its preparation the castle never saw any military action. Its one claim to fame came when Queen Isabella virtually ruled England from Castle Rising after she and her lover, Roger Mortimer, caused the murder of her husband, King Edward II, in 1327. (Remember Berkeley Castle?) Edward III finally seized power, executed Mortimer, and forced his mother into retirement.

If you are a worrier about white-collar crime ("pin-stripe crime" in Britain), pick up a book on British Royalty and read about some of their shenanigans. I'm referring to ages long past, not the recent rash of royal ruckus. At least the moderns aren't beheading each other.

ST. WENDREDA - ANGEL

MARCH

The "glory" of St. Wendreda's Church at March is its late fifteenth-century double-hammer-beam angel roof, "reputedly the finest in England." (I'm quoting from the rather extensive guide book). Evidence of two other buildings on the site have been discovered. One is documented in the Domesday Book, but the present church, built from rubble-stone, dates from the fourteen hundreds.

What, exactly, is a "double hammer-beam angel roof?" That was what we wanted to know.

In large rooms (I mean colossal) that had extra-high roofs pierced with clerestory windows, the walls had been known to collapse. Oak hammerbeams were designed to intercept the lateral thrust of pressure on the walls. The hammerbeams were then weighted near their base with heavy stone ornamentation for added stability. The idea soon went out of favor due to the great expense of engineering them.

63

And what about the angels at St. Wendreda's? There are one hundred and eighteen of them carved from oak, several half life-size, projecting "with wings outstretched" from the hammerbeams to gaze on the worshippers below.

Some folks might be struck with awe, reverence, disgust, or amazement, but St. Wendreda's squadron of angels peering from above gave me a good laugh. From the day I saw the church to later reading about it in the rather futzy pompous guidebook, the whole idea has rolled me in the aisle. The church is different, I'll say that for it.

I believe I forgot to mention that St. Wendreda's remains are interred in the churchyard.

CROYLAND ABBEY

Croyland was built in the Fens on land that was once desolate swamp. It was founded in AD 716 in memory of St. Guthlac, a distressed soul who had a need to get away from it all.

The official guidebook from the abbey states, "Many medieval monasteries claimed a greater antiquity and continuity than can be proven today." Aha! I have often been leery of these early abbey dates, and apparently I'm not the only one. The fact is that they cannot be traced absolutely in most cases. But it takes nothing away from the glory of the structures.

The history of Croyland includes several devastating fires. In fact it burned and had to be rebuilt three times. Buildings were wood instead of stone in Britain until about the eleventh century, and fire gutted many of the early castles and abbeys. What remains of Croyland today was built of stone in 1427.

A solid tower and ruined Norman arch look over a village of timber-framed cottages. The roofless Norman nave is a lovely spot for a few moments of personal reflection on the spectacular ruins from one of the wooden benches placed among trimmed lawns and rambling roses. The north aisle of the abbey church dates from the fifteenth century and is now a parish church.

STAMFORD

Stamford was recorded in the Domesday Book as "a town encircled by a medieval town wall." There is but one small spot where the wall remains today, but Stamford is still considered one of the finest medieval towns in all of Europe.

The wool trade was responsible for its heyday in the twelfth century, but by the sixteenth century the wool trade had declined, and the River Welland had silted up. Not to be shut out, the town began a busy trade catering to stagecoach travelers. Coaching inns took great care of their guests with comfortable beds, good food and drink. Today Stamford bustles with activity in and around many of those fine stone medieval buildings.

We found Stamford to be a great place to shop. We spent a good part of three days rambling through the stores and markets.

There are sketchy thirteenth-century castle remains near town. The castle belonged to one of the barons who forced King John to sign the Magna Carta at Runnymede in 1215.

One of the interesting things about Britain is that the ancient buildings are used heavily everyday. It is the citizens' way of life. They simply shrug it off if you mention historical importance in a way that suggests non-use. That does not mean there aren't plenty of well-educated people looking out for Britain's historical heritage. They recognize what they have and work constantly to make sure the weakest treasures are shored up, while the durable ones still withstand everyday use by the masses.

CASTLE ACRE

The hillside fortress village of Castle Acre once sat within the outer bailey of the castle for which it is named. Only fragments of the castle remain, but the visitor still shares a part of history by entering the village green through its impressive thirteenth century stone Bailey Gate. The castle, including extensive earthworks, was built over the old Roman road, Peddars Way. It s tracks still remain in places.

Houses and shops, built from castle stone, face onto the long narrow green lined with dramatically large and welcoming shade trees.

The Norman-ornamented ruins of a Cluniac priory dominate lawns at the edge of the village where the lofty, well-preserved front remains intact. A Tudor structure nearby called the Prior's Lodging is now a museum with relics from the priory.

BURGHLEY HOUSE

Burghley (Bur'-ley) is an extraordinary example of a showy country mansion with handsomely furnished rooms. It was built in 1552 in the Elizabethan tradition by William Cecil (Lord Burghley), who was Lord High Treasurer to Elizabeth I.

Inside is a vast collection of art—over seven hundred works—paintings by many British and European masters, and items made from wood, silver, glass, and pewter.

The kitchen is outrageously large and impressive with its collection of two hundred and sixty copper cooking pots, some of them monumental in size. One wonders how anyone could have handled them either on or off the stove. A kitchen of such great size is testament to the fact that hordes of guests could be served all at once during the house's important years.

From a distance the roofline rivals the skyline of most large cities. It is a towered, turreted, chimneyed conglomeration of shapes proudly proclaiming the owner's wealth. There are trim lawns and a rose garden.

We enjoyed touring this enormous country house filled with treasures, wondering all the while if a pair of rollerblades might not be an advantage considering the fact that the kitchen seemed miles from the dining and living areas.

OTHER THINGS TO SEE IN THE AREA

FELBRIGG HALL is a Jacobean house with an extensive library and an interesting collection of Dr. Samuel Johnson's manuscripts. We were impressed with a collection of old-world globes. GLORIA DEO IN EXCELSIS is carved in stone across the entire parapet on the south front.

HEYDEN is a small spread-out village from which the author, Barbara Pym, modeled some of her novels.

SHERINGHAM PARK is a rhododendron garden on the north coast of East Anglia. If you like rhododendrons this is the place for you.

DWIGHT
WILLIAMS
—WINDPUMP—WEYBOURNE.
No. NORFOLK COAST—

WINDMILLS (Windpumps they are sometimes called) were used for draining the extensive marshy fen country. The drainage of the fens began in Roman times but became more serious when the English hired the Dutch to do the job, the world's experts at draining wetlands.

Two beautiful cathedrals in the area are LINCOLN and ELY. Though they are not exactly neighbors, they are both worth a visit. Lincoln Cathedral is spectacular on its hill two hundred feet above the city. The Angel Choir at the front of the church holds the small carved stone figure of the notorious "Lincoln Imp". Ely Cathedral sports a very distinctive lantern tower. Also in Ely you'll find the interesting home of Oliver Cromwell.

NORTH ENGLAND

Traveling north, after you pass by the large industrial cities of Sheffield, Leeds, and Bradford, you drive into what amounts to a different country. The land seems to heave a great sigh of relief and stretches out before you in incredible wide-angled vistas. The topography changes—the country rolls in humps and swales, higher and higher, toward the Pennines and Dales in the west and out to the quaint fishing villages stepping down the steep, vertical cliffsides of the east coast where they are exposed to the moods of the North Sea. In between are lovely wooded valleys, jagged peaks, waterfalls gushing into rocky ravines, and desolate heather and gorse-covered Moors with their ancient trekking ridges.

The lifestyle changes. The population is sparser and the people are closer and flintier in their ways, less prone to travel any distance from home. The language, too, is different and more clipped. The English spoken in Yorkshire, Durham, and Northumberland was influenced by the Danes, while the southern part of the country came under Germanic influence.

It seems to us this region might reasonably be called Britain's 'Big Sky' country. As we shall see, there are fortified mansions, castles, and abbeys to remind us of the varied and fascinating history of England's north country.

NORTH YORKSHIRE

We first became interested in Yorkshire from watching the James Herriot series, *All Creatures Great and Small* on Public television. Could there really be a place left in the world as pastoral and medieval-looking as the show portrayed, or had the producers merely set up a location of fourteenth and fifteenth-century houses and barns in which to film the show? We had to know. The characters had become our friends through books and television.

What a pleasure it was to find that the village of "Darrowby" could be found in isolated spots all over the Yorkshire Dales.

North Yorkshire is the largest county in England. Wool is still a major industry. Fluffy black-faced, high-country sheep dot the hillsides in all directions. The farms are old and as solid as the stone barns, stark houses, and jagged wavy-lined walls that seem to run on in an endless pattern of ancient boundaries. The stacked dry-walls were built from stone cleared from the fields.

DWIGHT
WILLIAMS
— LANGTHWAITE, No. Yorks. —

row houses that step up a steep hillside to a mostly deserted town called Booze. (Yes, Booze!) The actress directed us down the road to the watersplash seen in the opening scenes of *All Creatures* where we took photographs of our car splashing through it.

While we were deep into our mental journey into the past, an RAF jet fighter split the air over our heads (the Yorkshire hills are their training ground), and we were reminded of how impossible it is to leave the modern world behind for any time at all.

LANGTHWAITE

This interesting little village, with its air of antiquity, lies midway up Arkengarthdale. Access to the village is over a humpback bridge that crosses Arkle Beck. This is the bridge the characters in *All Creatures* gaily whip across in their vintage car during the lead-in to the show, one of the main attractions on our first trip to North Yorkshire. We enjoyed driving over the bridge and taking photographs of rock-shingled homes along the beck.

On the town side of the bridge are a general store and several large grey-stone houses. While we wandered, we met a lovely young woman who had been an actress on a prominent BBC television drama. Her mother lived in one of the

REETH

As isolated as the village of Reeth is, it is one of the largest in Swaledale with stone-built houses and handsome grey-stone hotels, shops, and inns gathered around a well-kept village green. Cobbled parking areas add a further touch of romance. It was once the center of lead mining in nearby hills.

We always manage to pass through Reeth when we're in Yorkshire. It is where Swaledale and Arkengarthdale meet, so it becomes a touchstone of sorts. There is something gratifying about going back time and again to a place with which you have become familiar.

We once bought a map of Britain that turned out to have several mistakes and typos throughout. The first one we noticed was that they had left off the village of Reeth! How thoughtless!

THIRSK

One of the things that took us to this market town is that it was the home of the veterinarian and author, James Herriot, who, unfortunately, died while I was writing this book.

Thirsk is an ancient town that still holds its regular market days in the huge cobbled Market Square and probably helped to model the town of Darrowby in Herriot's novels. A handsome Victorian clock towers over the square.

As in other villages at the foot of the Dales, many coaching inns in Thirsk were stopovers for stagecoaches traveling the main route between Northern England and Scotland.

CURLEW

WENSLEYDALE HEIFER

In West Witton we sought refuge from a heavy rainstorm in the Wensleydale Heifer Inn. The inn dates from the seventeenth century. Three local couples had also escaped the storm and were having tea. A welcoming fire burned on the grate, the flames reflecting from the blue and white china collected on high shelves around the walls. The comforting warmth set the stage for strangers to become acquainted.

In our conversation, one of the ladies told us the story of Hannah Hauxwell, a woman of the Yorkshire Hills (due to boundary changes her home is in County Durham today), who had never married but had dedicated her life to caring for her sick family. When the last of them was gone, Hannah ended up a one-woman farmer on a remote Pennine farm with neither electricity nor running water, and all of this in relatively recent times.

There were several books about her life, *Season's Of My Life,* and its sequel, *Daughter Of The Dales,* written in cooperation with Barry Cockcroft who produced them for British television. The tale doesn't differ a great deal from the tales of early survival reported in the *Foxfire* books about the mountain folks in northern Georgia—mostly just a difference in location.

On our most recent trip we looked for Hannah Hauxwell's home called Low Birk Hatt, but we were never quite satisfied that we had found the right one. We did get a good idea of the location because we knew we were within the very neighborhood. Somehow the area didn't seem terribly remote to us, but we had to consider that many folks were poorer in the days between the First and Second World Wars, so they sometimes had to walk great distances for necessities. If they weren't up to it, they went without. Fortunately Hannah made enough money on her books to retire to a more comfortable life in nearby Cotherstone village.

DWIGHT
WILLIAMS.
—ATLAS FOUNTAIN
CASTLE HOWARD

CASTLE HOWARD

This exceptional country mansion was brought to our attention by Masterpiece Theatre's drama of Evelyn Waugh's novel, *Brideshead Revisited*. Much of the story was filmed there, and what a fit location for it!

The huge domed cupola appears above the trees long before the mansion comes into view. A narrow road meanders through acres of well-tended parkland until the creamy stone structure, looking like it could be an exceptionally fine state capitol building, spreads long tentacles before you and seems to have no end.

The main hall is seventy feet high with murals painted across the domed ceiling. Paintings by old masters line the walls between columns, with intermittent niches for ancient Greek and Roman statuary. The rooms are heavily ornamented with extravagant baroque furnishings.

The grounds are fit for any mansion. Weeping copper beeches, blood-red dancing silhouettes against jade-green lawns, are eye-catchers. We particularly enjoyed the magnificent high-spraying fountain of Atlas because we remembered several scenes in *Brideshead* that took place near it. We were at Castle Howard one morning at the moment the fountain was turned on. How dramatic!

CONEYSTHORPE, a village built specifically for those who serve Castle Howard, is charming with sturdily-built stone cottages around an attractive village green. From the green the visitor looks across the fields to a fine rear view of Castle Howard.

WHITBY

Whitby on North Yorkshire's east coast is a fishing port and seaside resort. It is most well known for Captain James Cook having set sail from its shores for Tahiti in his famous ship, the *Endeavour*, in 1768. There is a monument to Cook on the coast.

HOVINGHAM AND THE MALT SHOVEL PUB

Northwest of Castle Howard is the village of Hovingham. It is an impeccable village of sheep-dotted meadows and sturdy golden stone cottages. Its great tidiness is not accidental, for Hovingham is an estate village (caters to the Manor House folks at Hovingham Hall).

It was THE MALT SHOVEL PUB that we enjoyed—a delightful place for dinner. The food was exceptional and the innkeeper entertaining. We highly recommend it for an evening out while you're in the area.

Stiff rows of tall red brick houses, layer upon layer, move up the steep cliffsides strung together by narrow twisting lanes and steep flights of steps. From time to time through the centuries, raging seas have been known to wash away houses at sea level.

There are extensive abbey ruins high on the cliffs overlooking the sea. In town is a marine museum with mementos of Captain Cook and William Scoresby, a famous whaling captain.

PATRINGTON (Humberside)

Saint Patrick's Church merits a visit because it is England's "finest village church" (as announced on its entry porch). A lofty spire rising from a delicately-wrought stone tower may account for some of the parish's pride. Tall wide windows let more light inside than most village churches we've seen. The building is known for a fine timbered roof, many carved details, and a medieval rood screen across the chancel.

The members can rightfully be proud of the outside, too, for the building seems to have a perfectly-balanced design and welcoming shady grounds with lovely old stones covered with moss. If it isn't England's absolute finest, it must be near the top.

BEVERLEY MINSTER (Humberside)

Beverley Minster, Church of St. John the Evangelist, was started in 1220, and is considered a medieval masterpiece of Gothic design. The fine wood and stone carving throughout the building is worth the visit.

An interesting thing to look for is the stone "sanctuary chair" that dates from Saxon times. It sets near the altar. Historians believe a judge sat in the chair to hear pleas from fugitives who wanted to gain sanctuary in the church. The right-to-sanctuary was finally abolished, but fortunately the chair remained. An organ dating from 1767 still fills the building with beautiful music.

Beverley is a nice city with lovely Georgian buildings and two market days a week. A museum of Army Transport (WWII) may interest some.

OTHER THINGS TO SEE

You won't want to miss AYSGARTH FALLS in Wensleydale. There are several falls tumbling into each other from different heights, so a walk through wooded areas along the River Ure Gorge is in order to see the extent of this turbulent cascade.

All of the DALES are inviting drives. Besides Arkengarthdale and Swaledale, we have driven extensively

WHARFDALE

through Wensleydale, Coverdale, Nidderdale and Wharfdale. You'll be hard put to find more picturesque stone bridges, barns, and general pastoral scenery than you'll see in these lovely valleys.

From Wharfdale one can easily get to HAWORTH, actually in West Yorkshire and slightly southwest of Keighley. It was the home of the Bronte family. The fascinating thing about the place is that between the church and their rectory home is a mish-mash of headstones literally crammed in, perhaps with some graves piled on top of others. Stones that had been crowded out are lined against the fences. Studies indicate that several members of the Bronte family may have suffered untimely deaths as a result of polluted water from the graves.

Moving back north a ways is the town of HARROGATE. This is a typical Yorkshire town built around a large park in the city square. Pretty flower gardens and plenty of good shopping make this a popular place to visit.

THE CITY OF YORK AND YORK MINSTER is just east of Harrogate. In spite of the hordes of tourists, one should not think of leaving Yorkshire without a walk around York's MEDIEVAL WALL with its remaining Roman fragments, to enjoy the gardens that spill out below it. Another delight is a walk through the SHAMBLES, one of York's ancient shopping districts where black and whites have settled their upper stories out over the walk to nearly touch each other. The Romans started the city in 71 AD. Romans, Saxons, Vikings, Normans, and their successors have all left their mark on York.

YORK MINSTER is the largest Gothic cathedral in England and thoroughly dominates the city. It is one of the world's great examples of perpendicular Gothic architecture.

ABBEYS

Abbeys have been of keen interest to us for many years. It is not because we have a great new awakening that lands us in the middle of church activities, but because church and church-related buildings are a large part of world history and some of the most hauntingly beautiful and mysterious of man-made structures.

By the end of the twelfth century groups of Augustinians, Benedictines, Cistercians, and Gilbertines, as well as the more cloistered Carthusians and the more liberal Cluniacs, had built abbeys throughout England, Scotland, and Wales. The groups and their buildings were called by various names—abbeys, convents, priories, nunneries, friaries, hermitages, or monasteries. Each had its own priorities.

For instance, the most conservative were strictly cloistered and led lives devoted primarily to prayer and asceticism. Some served the parish churches while others were missionary groups. The nunneries, of course, were all women involved with the same type of activities. But when it all boils down, the groups had primarily the same objectives and engaged in the same activities to varying degrees.

At least twelve members were required to begin a new organization. Sometimes a group sadly dwindled to two or three lonely members before it was finally closed and those left were moved in with some other group. The ties to the abbey were quite strong—after all it was home—and movement to another group was often bitter and met with strong resistance.

Just as all members were to obey the same laws from day to day, it followed that the layout of their buildings should follow the same pattern. The churches, dormitories, refectories, and other domestic buildings each served a particular function. Every aspect of life was dictated by the centrally formed aims of the community, be it reclusive or public, for their support of each other's spiritual life was the essence of these groups.

Each organization developed a way to earn money for its necessities. It might be said that the communities served an economic purpose as well as religious. In fact, the wealthier groups were often the principle economic factor in their regions.

In 1533 Henry VIII took over the monasteries, made himself (instead of the Pope) head of the Church of England, and ordered the groups dissolved. Many of the buildings were partly or totally demolished. If the nave had been used as the parish church it was often saved.

Abbeys were abundant in Yorkshire. Here are four that we especially enjoyed and think they merit special attention.

BOLTON PRIORY

There is a great deal of charm merely in approaching the village of Bolton Abbey. The Augustinian Priory nestles in a remote and picturesque setting by the River Wharfe and has long attracted artists to its beautiful location. It was started in 1154.

The visitor enters the grounds through a small gateway into a parkland containing the abbey's remains—the nave and west tower—which serve as the parish church today.

On a nice day it is obvious that the people of this rather remote corner of Yorkshire use the extensive abbey grounds for family outings. As a place for a picnic it's hard to beat.

RIEVAULX ABBEY

Rievaulx (Re'-vo) was one of the most important Cistercian houses in the north of England because of its high total membership and for the beauty of the church. High grey stone arches are steeped in the lush green beauty of the heavily-wooded valley near the winding River Rye. Norman columns date to the founding in 1131.

The monks developed small furnaces to work local ironstone for their livelihood.

After the dissolution, when many of the monastic buildings were plundered for their dressed stone, Rievaulx somehow escaped nearly intact.

On the hill above the abbey is a well tended stretch of parkland called RIEVAULX TERRACE. It is a half-mile long grassy terrace washed in shades of green from handsome deciduous trees and rangy blooming shrubs. In amongst the shrubs on the cliffside are perfect spots for admiring and photographing the abbey ruins below. At either end of the terrace stands a small eighteenth-century temple.

MOUNT GRACE PRIORY

Here, near Northallerton, lived an austere order of Carthusian monks whose living arrangements were quite different from the other groups. The monks spent their time in separate cells and combined their way of life as solitary hermits with that of monks living in community.

They came together for the chanting of offices and met together in the Chapter House for business meetings, but the vast majority of their time was spent alone, praying and working in their cells.

The "cell" was a very small cottage of four rooms, a small private garden and privy. Lay brethren lived at the priory to wait on the monks, serving their food through tiny openings

DWIGHT
WILLIAMS
- MOUNT GRACE PRIORY -

in the cell wall so that nothing of their bodies could be seen. The visitor can clearly see how the separate cells were built with plenty of space around them for total privacy.

The ruins at Mount Grace are substantial, including some remains of the small priory church, and are quite beautiful in their secluded woodland setting.

DWIGHT
WILLIAMS
~ JERVAULX ABBEY ~

their job of holding up a long-gone roof, it has a welcoming restful atmosphere that many of the abbeys don't have.

I suppose its ambience is partly due to the massed purple aubrieta that tumbles over ruined grey stone walls in early summer banked against enormous clumps of wild yellow and white daisies that have no one to account to but themselves. This abbey is not as perfectly groomed as some and has fewer visitors, which gives us the feeling it may be more in keeping with its earlier days. But I have a hunch we enjoy the fact that nothing has happened there for four centuries. Ghosts of the past survive and one hesitates to disturb them.

One relatively modern touch, however, is a wooden bench upon which some feeling soul was moved to inscribe, "It is upon the Navy under the Providence of God that the safety and welfare of this empire depend."

One day, as we strolled the grounds peering into every corner, we stopped to stare at a neat row of stone sarcophagy laid out as though waiting...waiting. Some were hewn into ovals, some were shaped wide at the shoulders and narrow at the feet with a round flat hole for the headrest. There were several different lengths and widths. They were made in a time when death was a hard cold reality. There was no pretense made with silks and satins, artificial grass, or comfortable ruffled pillows and ivory comforters. I suppose we all feel slightly uneasy when our good times are abruptly interrupted by thoughts of death.

JERVAULX ABBEY

Jervaulx (pronounce this one Jar'-vis) was the home of a Cistercian group and is our favorite abbey. It was built in 1156. Small, with many beautiful arched passages and Norman columns still standing in sentinel rows after losing

Later we ran onto a group of stone sarcophagy at the Gilbertine Priory in Old Malton, a group that looked like they happily made mock of the grim business destined for them, like they had been tossed aimlessly against the wall by the hand of a humorous card sharp. Maybe the Gilbertines had a better sense of humor.

The Cistercians at Jervaulx made their way with the still-famous Wensleydale cheese. However, it was probably more famous for one of its abbots having led an unsuccessful rebellion against Henry VIII in the sixteenth century. The poor chap was imprisoned in the Tower of London and eventually hanged.

OTHER INTERESTING ABBEYS

The remains of FOUNTAINS ABBEY, a twelfth-century Cistercian house near Ripon on the River Skell is considered to be England's greatest monastic ruin, and it probably has the most visitors every year too. The exceptionally fine land-scaped garden of STUDLEY ROYAL, laid out in 1720, leads into the abbey and is actually an extension of the grounds. There is a seventeenth-century manor hall with a video film about the estate.

NUN MONKTON PRIORY northwest of York is a Benedictine nunnery founded in the twelfth century. It is a lovely isolated spot with unusual architectural features in the nave, which is still intact and used regularly by the village of Nun Monkton.

BYLAND ABBEY was the longest Cistercian church in England. The ruins of the west wall have the skeletal stone remains of a once-famous rose window. Medieval green and yellow tiles in geometric patterns pepper the floors in places and are fascinating for their preservation of color through the centuries. Byland is a large ruin but has fewer standing structures than some of the other abbeys.

HILL TOP FARM AT NEAR SAWREY (Cumbria)

"Peter Rabbit bought Hill Top Farm for Beatrix Potter in 1900." The saying is in keeping with the other childhood characters of Jemima Puddle-Duck, Tom Kitten, and Samuel Whiskers, all born at Hill Top Farm at the behest of the author's famous pen.

A stroll through the quaint farmhouse is fascinating because the visitor can see that the illustrations in her books came from scenes both within the house and outside the windows. At any moment one expects to catch a glimpse of the naughty Peter Rabbit peeking from behind plantings in the garden. The Tower Bank Arms pub down the hill behind Hill Top is recognizable from *The Tale of Jemima Puddle-Duck.*

The house is exactly what we would have expected from a woman who wrote children's stories. It is filled with graceful and feminine Victorian furnishings, homey hand-braided rag rugs, as well as collections of all sorts of small and dainty things. One room is dedicated to the author's memorabilia—handwritten correspondence to and from her editor, letters to friends about her writing, as well as watercolors that illustrate her books.

We like the way the front porch is built from four slabs of stone—two long ones on either side to form the walls, and two pieces that slant from the sides upwards to form a peak for the roof.

NEAR SAWREY is a pleasant quiet farm village, a perfect location for literary animals bent on getting into mischief.

GRASMERE (Cumbria)

William Wordsworth, probably the most universally known of the Romantic poets, spent fourteen years of his life in this village, eight of them at Dove Cottage. There are reminders of him everywhere in the village including a monument inside the Church of St. Oswald.

The white washed cottage, which had once been an inn, has been kept the way Wordsworth left it. In the early nineteenth century most poets had little financial security so it is not surprising that the poet's home was a humble one. Wordsworth loved the lake country and described Dove Cottage and grounds as a "Sweet garden-orchard, eminently fair,/The loveliest spot that man hath ever found."

One can easily see why he loved it so. It is a charming rambling house with pink and yellow roses clamoring over exterior walls and trellises. A neatly-built stone wall with clipped hedges behind it line the walk.

Nearby, a former blacksmith's shop has been made into a Wordsworth museum that houses a collection of the poet's important manuscripts.

TOWNEND FARM

This house at Troutbeck in Cumbria is not well known, but we found it to be an interesting example of a Lake District yeoman farmer's house. The building was started in the 1620s, but it is uncertain when different parts were built for it has undergone many changes and additions. There is heavy and richly carved oak furniture, and since the Browne family who lived at Townend for many generations was noted for not discarding anything, fascinating domestic items of the past are plentiful. The library contains some two thousand volumes. A barn and other outbuildings are interesting to explore.

We enjoyed the small but inviting garden of herbs and perennials as well as one of the best looking handmade twig gates we've ever seen (they're becoming popular in Britain as well as here). It enclosed the garden on one end.

DUDDEN VALLEY AND HARDKNOTT PASS

The Dudden Valley is a knobby, rocky area in the southwest of the Lake Country, leading north to Hardknott Pass—very steep with lots of mist and rain. The British don't bother to use switchbacks on steep roads like we do in this country, so you're faced with a thirty degree grade to climb. We found it to be more exhilarating than it was frightening. Going up I said needlessly, "This engine smells hot." Dwight grinned and said just as needlessly, "That's because this engine *is* hot." When we reached the top we gave our little car a rest while we admired the scenery.

Hardknott seems like a perfect name for a place so nearly inaccessible and remote, so high and wild. It is one of the lesser traveled roads in the area with an assortment of wild flowers and patches of colorful vegetation. Near the summit is HARDKNOTT ROMAN FORT, some three acres of ruins. You need to watch carefully for it. It's easily missed.

ary capital of the world! Eccentric designs—hats, human figures, animals, swoops, circles, squares, triangles, knots, and other sorts of tangles—danced before our eyes like a three-ring circus.

Fortunately the garden escaped the eighteenth-century craze for changed landscaping and remains today much as originally planned.

A collection of working model steam engines hiss and clank to life on Sundays.

OTHER THINGS TO SEE IN THE AREA

DENT is a remote and ancient village in Cumbria at the western edge of the Yorkshire Dales National Park. Cobbled streets are flanked by stone cottages, antique shops, art galleries, and the colorful George and Dragon Inn.

From Dent, move east to Hawes, then north up BUTTERTUBS PASS. This is an interesting area where the ground has sloughed away in spots from water erosion. To see the deep tubs (some as deep as a hundred feet), you must do some trekking near the summit.

ROMALDKIRK is a sheltered village in Teesdale, a few miles northwest of Barnard Castle. It has three village greens surrounded by houses set behind their own pretty gardens. An eighteenth-century coaching inn and a restored twelfth-century church are satisfying sites to explore.

LEVENS HALL

Levens is a grey-gabled Elizabethan house south of Kendal on A6. It began as a fortified tower house. Today the base of the tower is seen in the undercroft as a gift shop. In 1580, a series of lavishly decorated rooms was added which remain much the same today.

Our interest was in the amazing topiary garden laid out in 1690. Although we had read about it before we went, we were not prepared for what we saw. This has to be the topi-

ALNWICK CASTLE

From its inception, Alnwick (Ah'-nick) was larger than most castles. Originally a Norman castle stood on the site high over the River Aln. Although rebuilt in the fourteenth century, the castle still reveals the original Norman plan—a centrally-placed motte (a man-made hill for defensive purposes) surrounded by two curtain walls which enclose five acres.

In 1309 the castle was acquired by the Percy family and was turned into a rugged stronghold to keep the Scots from crossing the River. Many of the fortifications are similar to those castles in Wales of Edward I.

Even though the enormous rooms inside have been redone in elegant palatial grandeur, there is no doubt from the austere outer appearance that the castle was originally built for something other than peaceful luxury.

We found it to be an extraordinary castle because of its size and harsh massive display of medieval power. One whole Great Hall is devoted to an extensive collection of early

medieval armor and weaponry. A room dedicated to torture equipment quickly grabs the visitor's imagination.

The Percy family has resided at Alnwick for seven hundred years. Their North American family connections have resulted in some magnificently ornate Canadian pine ceilings in the Great Rooms.

DWIGHT
WILLIAMS
—LINDISFARNE CASTLE—

LINDISFARNE PRIORY AND CASTLE

Holy Island, off the coast of Northumberland, is a mysterious place partly because high tide covers the causeway and cuts it off from the mainland periodically, leaving the island remote, grey and desolate, with water birds screaming eerily overhead. Going to and from the island means you must know the times for the tides. They are published locally.

It may have been because of its remoteness that the Lindisfarne Priory was settled there by Benedictines in the eleventh century. There are extensive red-and-grey sandstone ruins. An earlier abbey ruled by St. Cuthbert had been on the site from the six hundreds but was sacked by the Danes in the ninth century. That early group produced the elegantly-decorated Lindisfarne Gospels now in the British Museum.

Lindisfarne Castle, started in 1550, was built from the grey stone of the earlier abbey as a bulwark against the invading Scots. It stretches across the peak of the only sizable rock formation on the island and looks toward the priory on one side and the North Sea on the other.

In 1902 Sir Edwin Lutyens made the fort over into a handsome castle home incorporating vaulted stone ceilings and hallways, and adding the warmth of wood beams and red brick floors. The rooms are furnished with Flemish and English oak pieces. The dining room is famous for a startling blue wall that seems to draw color favorably from the wood furnishings and oriental carpets surrounding it.

When we arrived at the castle we asked if we could use 'the loo' (restroom). We were directed to a stone wedge of a room with a long arrowslit for a window from which one looks straight down into the churning waters of the North Sea. The guide referred to it as 'the original loo with a view.'

The vast grounds are wild oceanside vistas save for one formal garden designed by the famous Gertrude Jekyll.

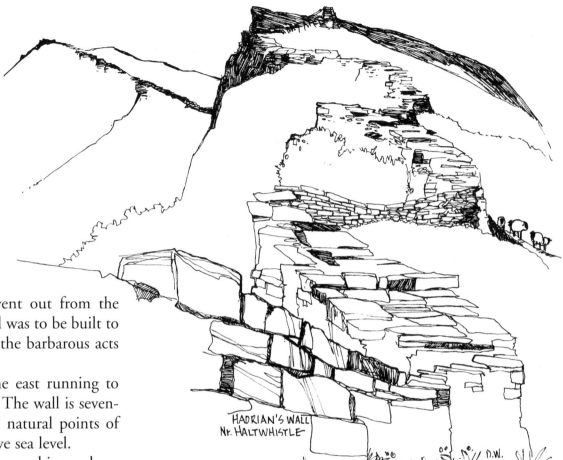

HADRIAN'S WALL
Nr. HALTWHISTLE

HADRIAN'S WALL

In the years AD 122-30 an order went out from the Roman Emperor Hadrian that a great wall was to be built to the north of England as a barrier against the barbarous acts of the Scots.

Beginning at Wallsend-on-Tyne in the east running to Bowness on the Solway Firth in the west, The wall is seventy-three miles long following the highest natural points of land, and at its highest was 1230 feet above sea level.

At least two attempts were made to move this northern frontier further north to a location in Scotland known as the Antonine Wall. These attempts failed and Hadrian's Wall stands as the chief monument to the final outpost of the Roman Empire. We have often joked that the Scots (the Picts in fact) were too wild and woolly for even the Roman Legions. Actually it's more than a joke. It is said that one Legion marched into Scotland and never returned.

The wall is stone and partial earthworks. Its western end was made of turf as an expedient to completion. The whole was originally twelve feet high and about twelve feet thick. There was a fort every mile with larger garrisons every few miles. When the Romans abandoned the wall in 383, the stone was removed as time went by to build villages, abbeys and farmhouses along its route, plus a new road from Newcastle to Carlisle. Today the wall is about four to six feet high.

We have spent both pleasant and rainy afternoons walking the wall, steeping ourselves in its history as we photographed the serpentine shape it follows as well as the rolling lush green countryside around it. As is usual, the wall is put to good use everyday to keep the sheep in.

SCOTLAND

Scotland is a tumbling rugged country. Mountains, often covered with snowy peaks, poke above much of the northern part. With sparkling blue lochs, tumbling mountain streams, and lush wooded valleys, we have often thought it has more than a little resemblance to the Pacific Northwest.

But when dark clouds gather, bringing heavy rain, the land is as filled with gloom and brooding as is much of its history. Then come the strong winds from the Atlantic Ocean to clean the sky, and a warm welcome sun ("a blaze-up") reveals velvety green moors and high slopes covered with heather.

As one moves out of England to the Border area in the south of Scotland, the topography changes to fertile fields and rolling grasslands mixed with high-country moors and rocky cliffs. Rich pasture land is speckled with sheep and cattle.

The language changes immediately too. When we first crossed the border into Scotland we happened onto a fisherman (complete with stalker cap) stalking salmon on the River Esk. While we visited with him, we were totally fascinated with his ability to effortlessly roll an *r* at length, and stretch an *a* to the point of making it an extra syllable.

When many of the Scots immigrated to America in the eighteenth century, they left behind homes—from cottages to castles—that were unique to their country. The cottages had dry-laid stone walls, earthen floors, and thatch or heather roofs, while the turreted rough-cast castles had come under French influence.

The River Tweed, the Cheviot Hills, and the Solway Firth form a common border between Scotland and England. Centuries ago it was a wild lawless border with the English trying to conquer Scotland. It was a long and difficult struggle. To add to the misery, rival clans fought bitterly among themselves over real or imagined slights, jealousies, and misunderstandings, often making life nearly intolerable.

The clans were active from 1000 A.D., and some feuded for centuries. The Johnstones and the Maxwells, for example. After their last battle near Lockerbie in 1593 (Yes, the Lockerbie where the plane went down), the Johnstones lopped off the defeated Maxwells' ears. Along the border the unsightly dreaded mark was dubbed "the Lockerbie nick." Most of the clans lost power after the rebellion of 1745.

It is no wonder the country seems filled with more castles, fortified houses, and battlegrounds than anything else. But each has its own history and the scenery of the modern rugged country of Scotland is beautiful to travel through.

Families who lived near the border were subjected to the hardships of constant raids from across the line in which they lost livestock, family furnishings, and sometimes family members.

Sir Walter Scott, who grew up on land near Smailholm, had spent his youth playing around the tower and was dramatically affected by its history. Tales told to him by his family imply that the Scots fought back fiercely, that they gave as good as they got. His feelings were made clear in a section of the poem "Marmion."

And still I thought that shatter'd tower
The mightiest work of human power;
And marvell'd as the aged hind'
With some strange tale bewitch'd my mind,
Of forayers, who, with headlong force,
Down from that strength had spurr'd their horse,
Their southern rapine to renew,
Far in the distant Cheviot blue,
And, home returning, fill'd the hall
With revel, wassel-rout, and brawl.
Methought that still with trump and clang,
The gateway's broken arches rang;
Methought grim features, seam'd with scars,
Glared through the window's rusty bars,
And ever, by the winter hearth,
Old tales I heard of woe or mirth,
Of lovers' slights, of ladies' charms,
Of witches' spells, of warriors arms;

In the summer lighthearted dioramas of characters from Celtic folklore are placed throughout the tower to charm the visitor.

SMAILHOLM TOWER

Nowhere in the Border Country is there a better example of the Scots trying to remain independent than at Smailholm Pele Tower. The Tower perches on a high rocky crag to allow a good view in all directions for safety's sake.

Seven-feet-thick walls are five stories high. Since any opening caused increased vulnerability to invasion by marauders, the windows were small and scarce, and for increased safety the family was quartered upstairs while guards kept watch below.

MELROSE ABBEY

Built of handsome local red sandstone, Melrose Abbey is a twelfth-century Cistercian ruin where the heart of Robert Bruce, a fourteenth-century Scottish king and national hero, is reputedly buried. Sheep farming produced the abbey's income. But like other border villages and abbeys it had the misfortune of being sacked regularly during the Border Wars between the English and Scots, finally falling into ruins.

Near the abbey, PRIORWOOD GARDEN offers two interesting specialties: scientific studies of an assortment of flowers grown for drying, and historic strains of apple, some from Roman times and others established by Melrose Abbey's early monks.

In the village, a motor museum may interest some. Paths on both banks of the Tweed, linked by a suspension footbridge, create a pleasant walk.

TRAQUAIR HOUSE

Traquair is a stark-looking Stewart stronghold (the oldest occupied house in Scotland) that stands in a coveted site in the upper valley of the Tweed. It housed Mary Queen of Scots and her second husband, Lord Darnley, from time to time. Its origins are medieval, but it was altered slightly in the seventeenth century and has not been changed since. Much of its contents date from the medieval period.

A secluded library slumbers peacefully while an intellectual frieze of ancient philosophers looks on. The books have not been rearranged on the shelves for two hundred years.

TRAQUAIR HOUSE.

A black lace dress that Mary, Queen of Scots, had worn to prayer is laid out on one of the beds. The chapel where she prayed is beautiful and includes a priest's hole with a secret escape staircase, a necessity in times of religious turmoil.

Since the Civil War in 1645, the Stewarts, who were Roman Catholics, had not been allowed to hold Catholic services. Legend has it that after several Catholic uprisings and the arrest and incarceration in the Tower of London of several of the Stewarts (the English spell it Stuart), a pair of gates with bears on the posts on Traquair property were locked by order of Bonnie Prince Charlie and were not to be opened again until the Catholic Stewarts were restored to the Scottish throne. That never happened so the gates remain locked today.

There are other legends about the locking of the gate, all having to do with the restoration of Stewarts to the throne, but this one seems most feasible.

Other treasures of Traquair include historic documents, china, needlework done by the Scottish Queen, and a harpsichord that dates to 1651.

Attached to the main house is an eighteenth-century brewery where Traquair homemade ale is bottled and sold.

DRUMLANRIG

A painting by Rembrandt, "An Old Woman Reading," is one important attraction at this country estate built in the seventeenth century. But the house itself is an attraction. Fifteen lead-capped turrets give it an air of confident haughtiness.

It contains many other art treasures. Among them are original paintings by John Singer Sargent, unique pieces of silver, and many fine pieces of French furniture. But we thought Rembrandt's famous painting outshone them all.

CAERLAVEROCK CASTLE

This triangular-shaped stronghold of the Maxwells is just slightly southeast of Dumfries near the border. It is the only triangular castle in Britain, and seems oddly out of proportion with its thick, blocky thirteenth-century gatehouse gloating over the rest like a cat with a cornered mouse. There was an outer moat around the castle (gone now), earthworks, then another moat, forcing attackers to cross two bridges before they got to the well-guarded gatehouse. One moat remains, but it seems almost like a garden water feature rather than a military necessity.

The castle had a turbulent history. Edward I captured it for England, but his men declared loyalty to the Scots so the castle had to be routed again. Whereupon the Scots retaliated and destroyed it. All in all, the castle was captured, destroyed, and rebuilt three different times.

In the seventeenth century, along came an Earl who had the courage to rebuild the castle again to its original plan, creating a mansion of reputed magnificence within the battlemented walls. But the travails were not over. Soon after the mansion was completed it was sacked by the Covenanters and finally left in ruins. Yet, in spite of the strife, there are plenty of provocative ruins left to see.

- THE KING & QUEEN AT GLENKILN -

GLENKILN

North of Dumfries is a three-thousand-acre moorland and wooded estate turned into a sculpture garden with pieces by Henry Moore, Jacob Epstein, Auguste Rodin, and other lesser-known sculptors, at least lesser known to us.

We spent a good part of a day studying pieces near the road and hiking the country to find the sculptures tucked away in wooded areas. We didn't have time to see the whole collection but we enjoyed the ones we found. Our favorite was "The King and Queen" by Henry Moore. The characters are more than life size and obviously symbolic. They gaze over a picturesque lake from a bench on the hillside.

Our suggestion is to give yourself plenty of time if you enjoy sculpture and want to see the full collection. Since we saw Glenkiln, we have read about several other estates taking up similar plans.

GRETNA GREEN

Gretna Green Hall is an old border hotel well known from the past for legalizing weddings simply if the couple made a declaration before witnesses. In England couples had to be twenty-one years of age to marry, but in Scotland they could marry at any age.

Many runaways took advantage of the services. Often the parents of youths tried to have the marriages annulled, but they were legal in Scotland as far back as 1792. However, the legality of this kind of marriage ended in 1940.

The building, built in 1710, was once a tollhouse and smithy. Although creaking and groaning with age and a "gracious lack of upkeep," the place makes the most of its past with many early pin-up photographs of Hollywood and British film stars and mementos of other famous people who were married there. We found it interesting that we recognized so many faces.

The idea is still nostalgically appealing. Over a thousand couples "of legal age" seek out Gretna Green every year for their marriage ceremony.

OTHER THINGS TO SEE IN THE SOUTH OF SCOTLAND

KELSO is an elegant town with cobbled streets and a large open square with coaching inns. It s Benedictine abbey is now in ruins as a result of an order from Henry VIII that Scottish border villages be "tormented and occupied as much as they can be." FLOORS CASTLE is on the edge of town. It has a collection of fine tapestries, porcelain and paintings.

ST. ABB'S - a steep descent to this fishing village clinging to the cliffs on the east coast is rewarding. Volcanic outcroppings tower over a village of colorful fishermen's houses and fishing boats loaded with nets and lobster creels. A path

ST. ABBS . SCOTLAND

along the cliffs allows a precipitous walk to ST. ABB'S HEAD with a dramatic view of the North Sea. There is a lighthouse and a wildlife reserve.

JEDBURGH ABBEY suffered several sackings by invading armies—a price paid by being near the English-Scottish border. Little has survived but the church which has been restored in recent years. It is especially known for a magnificent west door. The town rivals Kelso in elegance.

ABBOTSFORD - Sir Walter Scott bought the many-turreted house in 1811 and lived there until his death in 1832. There are large collections of weapons and relics of Scott's life, a huge library, as well as a formal garden around the house.

BLACKNESS CASTLE is a stark bleak-looking castle on the Firth of Forth. It is surrounded by water on three sides. It seems a natural spot for use as a prison in the fifteenth century.

EDINBURGH has long been the capital of Scotland. There are many fine sights to see—Edinburgh Castle, Holyrood House, museums and monuments of all sorts. After you've seen these, again, we encourage you to get out of town and enjoy the countryside.

CASTLE
CAMPBELL.

CASTLE CAMPBELL

From the parking lot, a walk downhill on steep paths through wooded country is an appropriate approach to this isolated stronghold of the Campbells of Argyll. The grey stone fortress, with its lofty square tower, must have once been a chilling sight (it still is), perched precariously on a shrubbery-lined ledge over the Burn (creek) of Sorrow and the Burn of Care. A horseshoe of natural trees and shrubs encompass it, while hills scarred with brown patches of bracken sweep dramatically into the air behind it.

Long dark passageways lead into vast caverns. It s original name, Castle Gloom, gives the visitor pause for reflection. The unhappy names swirling about the place may have come from the Campbell clan's reputation among other clans. Scottish lore claims "there was nary a battle fought in Scotland that didn't have a Campbell at the bottom of it." For whatever the reason, the Campbells had the name changed to Castle Campbell by an Act of Parliament in 1489.

In 1650 the English occupied the castle for a short time, then set it afire and left it abandoned. The buildings surrounding the tower slowly fell to ruins, but the impressive stone tower surrounded by high massive walls remains today.

We suggest visitors allow themselves plenty of time for a fairly lengthy walk from the parking lot and a quiet savoring of some beautiful Scottish scenery.

THE ROYAL PALACE OF FALKLAND AND GARDENS

The palace was built in 1501 on the slopes of the Lomond Hills, replacing buildings from the twelfth century.

It had been the country residence of Stewart kings and queens who had brought guests to vacation and hunt in the Forest of Fife since the thirteenth century. Mary, Queen of Scots, spent the happiest days of her tragic life there.

The buildings are French Renaissance, small-roomed and ornate, with heavy bars to keep out invaders. Flemish and French artisans carved angels and medallions on the east range. A handsome oil portrait of the Scottish Queen hangs over the fireplace in the Queen's Room. The palace was redone inside in 1635 and lost many of its original furnishings and decorations. Some of those original pieces have been sought out and reclaimed.

There are lovely gardens and orchards laid out in a formal pattern behind the house along with the oldest Royal Tennis Court built in 1539. The court is designed to play a form of tennis using the walls and roof, not unlike the bank shots of our modern racquetball. The palace still belongs to Her Majesty, the Queen.

SAINT ANDREWS

You may have an argument on your hands if you try to suggest that Saint Andrews was ever good for anything but a golf course. Historians lament the fact that the village is known throughout the world only for its Royal and Ancient Golf Club which sets the rules for the game. The golf course surely is well known, but the medieval village is steeped in other kinds of history as well.

Old houses built from grey and golden stone taken from what was once the largest and one of the most elaborate cathedrals in Scotland line the streets. The cathedral has moldered in ruins on the east edge of town since the reformation, its dramatic remains creating an unavoidable backdrop.

The oldest university in Scotland, founded in 1410, is located there.

Cobbled streets contain crosses marking the graves of covenanters tortured by the Earl of Monmouth after the Battle of Bothwell Bridge in 1679.

Now, back to trying to get out of the Road Hole bunker...

DWIGHT
WILLIAMS
- LOCH TUMMEL -

TUMMEL FOREST AND LOCH

On the north bank of LOCH TUMMEL is some of Scotland's grandest mountain scenery. Queen Victoria visited in 1866, lending her name to one of the viewpoints. Signs along the way identify the mountains by name.

Stop at the car park to find forested walking trails. Scotland's wooded areas are as quiet and beautiful as any for a peaceful stroll.

Near the parking area an eighth-century ring fort is clearly marked. It offers spectacular views of the Loch, while a seventeenth-century farm settlement, now restored, is a fine spot for a picnic overlooking the scenery.

At the west end of Loch Tummel is KINLOCH RANNOCH, a village of stone houses with Virginia Creeper and climbing roses scattering color in all directions. From the village the visitor can view a waterfall that plummets from Mt. Beinn a' chuallaich into the River Tummel.

Beyond Loch Tummel is the larger and also scenic LOCH RANNOCH.

SCENIC DRIVE FROM BLAIRGOWRIE TO BRAEMAR

From Blairgowrie, the drive north to Braemar is marked on the map as one of the loveliest of scenic drives in Scotland, and it richly deserves the title.

Rolling rocky hills covered with heather, undulating grasslands, and clear-water burns tumbling from the heights, delight the traveler moving north from the Bridge of Cally through GLEN SHEE.

The day we drove the route the air was vibrantly clear and sunny. We parked in a scenic spot in Glen Shee and had lunch while we watched dozens of hang gliders plunge like injured birds from high cliffs, only to gain control on the air currents and soar with dignity above our heads.

As we moved along CLUNIE WATER we stopped at an inn for tea. We were surprised when we went inside and found the place rocking with deafening guitars and a wailing country music singer from Louisiana. Young people lounged wall to wall. We decided to head on up the road and find a quieter spot.

We found what we were looking for—a quaint little cow barn that had been turned into a tea shop and craft gallery. We will always remember the tasty piece of gingerbread, heavy with molasses and dusted with powdered sugar, that a dedicated farm wife served us.

North of Glen Shee the road along Clunie Water leads into BRAEMAR where there is a small, but exquisite, baronial castle. The Highland Games are held on the grounds, bringing a host of Highlanders and the Royal Family together for competitive sports and entertainment each September. The games, which had their origins in medieval war, have continued one place or another with few interruptions since the eleventh century.

BARONIAL CASTLES

In an area as small as Britain, things seem to come together in clusters—abbeys, battlegrounds, or military castles, for example. The same is true of northern Scotland's baronial castles. From Glamis Castle north to Cawdor, there are many of them marked on your map, each with its own history. We mention the following group because we have visited and enjoyed them. See them all, or pick and choose.

CRATHES CASTLE

Many of the Scottish castles were influenced by the French baronial style of architecture complete with turrets and battlements. Crathes, started in 1553, fits this style perfectly. One wing was destroyed by fire in 1960, but has been faithfully replaced like the original.

This is a homey and comfortable castle save for the steep spiral stairs carved out of stone walls. They're uneven and treacherous. One wonders how servants carrying heavy loads managed them without broken legs or ruptured discs. Still, the fun of a sightseeing trip like this is to see and experience the unusual. A baronial castle certainly offers a different view of life from our own.

Crathes has famous painted ceilings with biblical texts inscribed in them, and, as is true in many castles and old houses, one of the rooms is reputedly haunted.

The garden is enhanced by avenues of lime trees and trimmed yew hedges which divide the plantings into areas, each with its own plant varieties. Unusual topiary sets off the garden from the house to fine advantage. Topiary, it seems to us, is both zany and fun. Crathes's large topiary hedges are as zany as any.

CRAIGIEVAR CASTLE

This fairy tale castle beguilingly commands a hillside on the edge of the highlands in Aberdeenshire. It was built in 1626 for the Forbes family. The castle is fortified, but was intended from its inception for family rather than military life.

There are vaulted ceilings of intricately molded plaster throughout the interior. A bold blue, tan, and brown Scottish plaid carpet in the Great Hall and numerous hunting trophies on the walls give the house a festive air.

But there is a touch of the ominous. On the ceiling in one of the childrens' bedrooms is the inscription, "Doe not vaiken sleiping dogs" (Do not waken sleeping dogs), the motto of Craigievar. I don't know exactly what the motto meant, and I'm not sure I'd be willing to tease the bears to find out. One person suggested it may have had to do with the children—that they often turned against their parents to gain the family wealth. Did the parents fear them? We'll never know.

As befits a castle, Craigievar is said to be haunted. A young lady of the family, who was about to be married, had left a wedding invitation addressed "to the ghost of Craigievar" on the mantel in the Great Hall.

The grounds have a flavor of their own with informality the rule. An attractive round stone garden house (probably once a malt house) with a cone-shaped roof looms at the end of a stone wall near the house. In the summer, blooming bergenia thrives at its base. Other plantings are simple with an emphasis on carefully-placed copper beech trees flashing touches of red amid long sweeps of variegated green woods and well-trimmed lawns.

CAWDOR CASTLE

The fame of Cawdor Castle has rested largely on a bit of folklore—that it was the location of the murder of Scotland's King Duncan (according to Shakespeare) at the hand of Macbeth. Not true. Cawdor Castle was built in 1372, more than three hundred years after Duncan reigned (1034). Historians believe Macbeth of Moray, who had a claim to the Scottish throne by right of his wife, did indeed kill Duncan, but in a battle near Elgin, Scotland.

Through the centuries the castle has been slowly changed into a mansion to accommodate modern family life, and with an eye to escaping its bloody reputation.

But the building has an ominous unapproachable look, even today, from its turreted central tower to the thick-stoned, small-windowed walls that make up the rest of the living quarters. The visitor crosses a drawbridge over a deep moat and passes through an iron yett (protective gateway grille) that still guards the castle's entrance. Campbells of Cawdor have inhabited the castle since the late twelfth century.

Inside, ancient Flemish tapestries cover the walls along with many family portraits and other family relics. Outside, a well-designed flower garden blazes with bright yellow, red, and white blooms, lending a happier mood to the grey stone fortress.

D.W.

CAWDOR CASTLE.

GLAMIS CASTLE

A mass of chateau-like turrets, parapets, wings, and gables were added to this towering red-stone castle in the seventeenth century, giving it an aura of wealth and great importance. Important, indeed! From the fourteenth century Glamis has been the original home of the Lyons, the family of the present Queen Mother. She and her granddaughter, Princess Margaret, were both born there.

A sealed room inside said to be haunted by an Earl who played cards with the devil on the Sabbath is one of the castle's curiosities. Outside there are Dutch and Italian gardens and many fine tree species.

DRUM CASTLE

The hefty cube of a stone tower, built in the late twelve hundreds, is one of the three oldest in Scotland. We thought this was a beautiful small castle with lovely comfortable furnishings and one of the prettiest kitchens we have ever seen—blocky-sandstone floor, blue and white porcelain dishes on open shelves, ancient copper cooking pots hanging from well-used pegs, and a handsome long oak table heavily grooved from servants' use. A nicely-arched partition with interesting stonework separates the main part of the kitchen from the heat of the massive black-iron cooking stove.

The grounds contain ancient oak trees and other deciduous plantings.

13c. Tower
Drum Castle

BRODIE CASTLE

Brodie is an enormous white castle built in 1567. There have been buildings on the grounds occupied by Brodie's for eight hundred years. This castle was of interest to me since it carries one of my family names. However, my grandmother never lived in a house like this!

There is a notable collection of oil and watercolor paintings ranging from the early seventeenth through the nineteenth centuries. Inviting wood tones in period furnishings, unusual floor-to-ceiling four-sided bookshelves, and elaborate plaster-work ceilings create a distinctive interior. The present Laird of Brodie welcomed us, proud and resplendent in his Brodie-tartan kilt. We enjoyed that.

CULLODEN D.W.

CULLODEN

The history of the Scots' duel with the English crown over their independence was a long and bloody one. Nowhere is it more evident than at Culloden Moor just east of Inverness. Here the military struggle came to a tragic end.

History claims there was a stiff gale blowing the day the Stewart armies of Scotland and the English forces commanded by the Duke "Butcher" of Cumberland met in the last fierce clash in 1746. The clash was swift and bloody.

It took only an hour for government troops to clear out the five thousand Highlanders, leaving a thousand dead littering the field.

Small, rustic stone-marked graves of the dead Scots pock the field. Crude carving names a clan whose men lie in that spot, or is simply marked "mixed clans." The main part of the battle zone is clearly outlined with stones, even where the opposing commanders stood when the battle began, while flags of both sides fly to mark their lines. A memorial cairn maintains a grim reminder.

The visitor's center shows an audio-visual display, bringing a recount of the battle vividly to life.

GLENCOE. D.W.

GLENCOE

In spite of its infamous reputation for a clan massacre, Glencoe, just south of Fort William in the Highlands, is another of Scotland's most beautiful scenic drives. Although the mountains in the area average less than four thousand feet—not impressive by western American standards—they rise suddenly from sea level and seem dramatically high as they drop into steep treeless canyons.

Leave the roads and paths behind to enter untamed wilderness. The area is known for its rolling country comprised of some of the oldest outcroppings of rock in the world, rugged glowering mountain peaks often blanketed with mist, and some of the finest mountain climbing and walking country in the Highlands.

The spot where the MacDonalds were massacred by the Campbells in 1692 is marked with a tall stone cross in the lower part of the glen. Because of the massacre the area is often referred to as the Glen of Weeping. Pipers play regularly (and mournfully) from the hills in remembrance of the tragic event. "Remembrance" turns into something fairly lucrative, for the piper we happened onto had his music case spread out before him. It was overflowing with cash donated from passersby.

Fourteen-thousand-two-hundred acres of this historic site are in the care of the Scottish National Trust and are kept open to the public year round. There is a gift shop and a visitor's center with audio-visual materials.

DUNNOTTAR CASTLE

The dramatic ruins of Dunnottar are perched on top of a rocky cliff a hundred-and-sixty-feet above the restless North Sea with a truly spectacular view in all directions. The castle dates from the fourteenth century and was the location of bitter battles with the Crown.

Simply eyeing the place on the walk down the long open path to the gate sets one back in history to a time when coastal castles were "lean and mean." Scotland's crown jewels were hidden there from Cromwell's troops, but, as the tale goes, a local minister's wife smuggled them out in a basket of food and buried them beneath the floor of her husband's church, later to be secretly moved to Edinburgh where they remain today.

The castle was dismantled after the Jacobite rebellion of 1715. Still, there are plenty of ruins left to explore.

OTHER THINGS TO SEE IN SCOTLAND

WOOLLEN MILLS - You'll find many woollen mills scattered over Scotland's countryside. Some are working mills that show how the wool is spun into yarn, while others only sell sweaters and other woollen items. Consult your map in each area.

LOCH NESS - The choppy waters of Loch Ness are deeper than much of the North Sea, running to a depth of seven-hundred-fifty-four feet. A rift split Scotland along the Great Glen some four hundred million years ago forging the lochs. Then came glaciers ten thousand years ago to rearrange the countryside into wooded slopes and towering mountainsides. The waters of Loch Ness are often dark with brooding mists—a perfect spot for an elusive monster.

DISTILLERIES of the famous Scotch whisky are located along the River Spey that runs through Grantown. There are a number of them, so a tour might take some planning time-wise.

JOHN O'GROATS - We set out one day to drive to this little settlement near the northern tip of Scotland where the view north to the Orkneys is said to be outstanding. It is named for a Dutch family named De Groot that first settled the area. We got as far as Wick on the east coast. The weath-

er was so miserable with high winds and driving rain that we were finally forced south again.

We had planned to take a ferry to the Outer Hebrides the same week, but the weather had forced even the Minch boatmen to shut down. We ended the week south in the Cotswolds rambling through romantic golden-stone villages. It was a wonderful opportunity to explore niches of country-side we had not seen before.

TRAVELING TIPS

AUTOMOTIVE

The British drive on the left side of the road from the right side of the car, so remember, you must shift gears with your left hand. Avoid the problem by renting a car with an automatic transmission. It pays off in tight or stressful situations. Review the basic road signs before you take a rental car on the road. Your road map will itemize them for you.

Rent a car with a trunk that allows your luggage to be hidden when you lock up and leave it. This helps deter thieves when they don't see anything to take.

When you come to a sign with your highway number in parentheses, (A39) for instance, it means that you are not now on that road, but the road you're traveling leads to it.

There are seldom parking spots by the door of your destination. Use the parking lots located on village and town perimeters. Besides, you'll see more while walking through a village than you will while driving through it.

Don't poke along in traffic. If you need to consult a map, stop at the side of the road. The British have little patience with indecisive drivers and those who don't obey the law. Remember that you can stay on a roundabout and circle it more than once while you look for your destination on road signs that lead away from it. Passing lanes are meant for passing only. No matter what your speed, move to the left (slow lanes) as far as you can except to overtake another vehicle. None of this American habit of always driving in the passing lanes or passing on the wrong side.

When driving on a one-track road, an oncoming car may flash his lights at you. He's not mad, he simply means that he has stopped in a spot where you can pass first, so you go ahead.

FOOD

If you're traveling on a budget, as most of us do, pubs are your best bet for the evening meal. Ask your host or hostess which is best for dinner, and make sure you know what time the pub begins to serve. They vary on such things as which

night the cook is off, which day of the week the pub closes, etc. Order at the bar. Stay in the bar to eat instead of going to the dining room (if they have one.) The meals are the same, but less expensive that way. Occasionally you may be ushered from the bar to a dining room when your meal is ready. This is okay, same price.

Save by grocery shopping and eating lunch on the road. Take along a can opener, a sharp knife, and a butter knife for spreading. Buy bottled water for the car.

MONEY

Use credit cards whenever possible. You get the best exchange rate when the bill comes into the U.S. prior to exchange. More people will accept Traveler's checks in British Pounds than they will in American dollars. Buy pounds at the bank before you leave.

Stop at the airport money exchange booth to have a few pounds in your pocket on arrival in Britain.

Check on your insurances, both car and health, before you leave. Some bank cards and auto travel clubs give discounts and insurance coverage on foreign car rentals. Some health insurances don't cover bills overseas. You'll want to be sure you're adequately covered in all areas.

PASSPORT

Apply several months in advance for your passport. *Never check it through in your luggage. Keep it on your person at all times.* You'll need it when you do any kind of banking, enter and leave both the U.S. and Britain, as well as other times when you least expect it.

MAPS

Go to a good book shop and buy a detailed map—about four miles to the inch—with historic and scenic sites clearly marked on it.

PHOTOGRAPHY

Take along enough film for the trip. Film in Britain is very expensive. While you're in your local camera shop buy a lead bag to protect your film from airport scanners.

Photographs are prohibited inside most historic houses. If in doubt, ask. You can usually buy slides of interiors in the house's gift shop. If you want prints, colorful postcards is the

best way to go. Take a log book along to keep track of photos. While you may think you'll remember everything you photographed, chances are you won't.

Keep your photo equipment as simple as possible. You probably will have your camera with you most of the time, so saving weight is important. And changing lenses is clumsy and time consuming. Zoom lenses eliminate much of this. We try to maintain an awareness that not everyone is taking photographs or appreciates photographers, so don't be a photographic nuisance.

CLOTHING

Take only what you know you'll wear. There's nothing fun about lugging too-heavy suitcases. Besides, the car you rent may be small.

It rains off and on in Britain. A plastic raincoat with a hood beats an umbrella.

MEDICATIONS

Take along any medications you must take regularly, even over-the-counter drugs. They don't have the same drugs or trade names that we have in the U.S.

If you depend on eye glasses, take an extra pair just in case you break or lose yours. There is no way to replace them short of making an appointment to see an eye doctor—good luck!

MANOR FARMHOUSE
FLISHINGHURST. KENT

BED & BREAKFAST

Check the tourist information centers. Sometimes it is only a bulletin board in a park, but they're usually reliable. Often B & B signs are displayed on the property near the roads. Some areas have more than others. If you have trouble finding a B & B, small inns and hotels are a possibility. Large country inns and lavish hotels are expensive, so it pays to try to find a Bed and Breakfast. You'll get the hang of it. It's usually easier than you think and sometimes you'll happen onto a real jewel.

MISCELLANEOUS

Since Britain uses direct electric current, a plug adapter is a necessity for small appliances such as hair dryer, shaver, etc. Any small hardware store in a sizable village will have one.

FIELD- HOUSE
CUMBRIA

We always take a notebook to keep track of our itinerary. Later we refer to it often for details and facts about where we've been and what we did there.

You'll find a small flashlight helpful when you're sleeping in strange places—maneuvering hallways, bathrooms, etc., in the dark.

A soft collapsible bag that fits in the bottom of your suitcase may prove helpful in bringing home purchases. We put breakables in our hard bags and stuff the extra bag full of laundry and other clothing. Check the softie through on the airline with your other luggage on the way home.

If you're going to see quite a few National Trust properties it pays to buy a membership at the first site you visit. You'll save yourself many pounds.

TEESDALE

Opening and closing times of various historical sites are subject to change, which is why we didn't include them in this book. Ask your Bed and Breakfast host or hostess for information pamphlets. They all have them.

Remember, any trip should be three-fold fun: planning, doing, and remembering.

Artist's Notes

My decision to use line drawings in this book came, in part, because the subject is Britain, and the British have a greater continuing appreciation for black and white drawings than we in the United States have.

As there seems to be a renewed interest in black and white photography, maybe, in a small way, this book can help rekindle a sensitive awareness in black and white drawings.

After years of painting watercolors, I had to hone old skills with pen and ink. In my youth we did a lot of pen and ink drawing, dipping a pen point into a bottle of ink every line or two. I am grateful for the advances that have developed long-lasting, free-flowing instruments in a variety of shapes and widths.

I have found black and white drawings somewhat addictive. It's hard to stop putting clean black strokes on a smooth white surface. As the work on this book came nearer to an end, I kept wanting to draw more and more. But there comes a time when it's too late, at least for this project.

As any artist would have to admit, I have my favorite type of subject. I hope it doesn't show too much, but I'm sure I get just a bit more satisfaction from the pieces with architectural forms. The drawing of the Guild Hall at Lavenham, or the Arundel interior are good examples.

Humorous thoughts floated in the background during some of the scenic drawings. I kept thinking while drawing the permanently wind-twisted tree on the north Cornish coast how the politicians in Cornwall should certainly have no trouble knowing which way the wind blows. While drawing the garden and pond at Bateman's, I kept remembering how the Kiplings had a special designation in their guest book (still on display). "FIP" is written beside some names. It means "fell in pond."

The subjects of some of my drawings have already been paintings. No doubt others will be paintings in the future. But I have rediscovered the pleasure of a line drawing.

WEOBLEY AND
·SALUTATION
INN·

DWIGHT
WILLIAMS

INDEX